P9-BBN-142

HAMILTON
BOOK OF
Everything

Everything you wanted to know about
Hamilton and were going to ask anyway

Kim Arnott, Marvin Ross and Cheryl MacDonald

MACINTYRE PURCELL PUBLISHING INC.

Copyright 2008 by MacIntyre Purcell Publishing Inc.

All rights reserved. No part of this book covered by the copyrights hereon may be reproduced or used in any form or by any means — graphic, electronic, or mechanical — without the prior written permission of the publisher. Any request for photocopying, recording, taping, or information storage and retrieval systems of any part of this book shall be directed in writing to the Canadian Reprography Collective, 379 Adelaide Street, West, Suite M1, Toronto, Ontario, M5V 1S5.

MacIntyre Purcell Publishing Inc.
232 Lincoln St., Suite D
PO Box 1142
Lunenburg, Nova Scotia
B0J 2C0
(902) 640-3350
www.bookofeverything.com
info@bookofeverything.com

Cover photo istockphoto
istockphoto: page 6, 8, 50, 72, 138, 188
123RF: page 88

Printed and bound in Canada.

Arnott, Kim
Hamilton Book of Everything: everything you wanted to know about Hamilton and were going to ask anyway / Kim Arnott, Marvin Ross and Cheryl MacDonald.

ISBN 978-0-9784784-6-9
1. Hamilton (Ont.). 2. Hamilton (Ont.)--Miscellanea. I. Ross, Marvin II. MacDonald, Cheryl, 1952- III. Title.

FC3098.35.A76 2008   971.3'52
C2008-903298-5

Introduction

Okay, I'll own up to it right here — this book really doesn't have everything. No book ever could. One of the biggest challenges encountered by our team of writers and researchers was not what to put in but rather what to leave out. In the end, I hope we've included enough of everything to offer readers a fascinating, fun-filled snapshot of this complex, and sometimes contradictory city we call home.

Hamilton has many faces. The one that presents itself to the world along York Boulevard is considerably different than the one peering out along Burlington Street. We are both an industrial powerhouse and a uniquely-blessed area of natural beauty.

We are a city that revels in its lunchbucket mentality, despite the wealth of science, talent and innovation found within our borders. We are a city that celebrates both Boris Brott and hard-hitting Ti-Cat linebackers. We are a city that has spawned brilliant scientists, hilarious comedians, successful businesspeople and unforgettable politicians. Our diversity is both astonishing and inspiring, and offers the promise that Hamilton will thrive into the future.

This book was a team project. Marvin Ross, Cheryl MacDonald and I were the writers and researchers responsible for the content, while Kelly Inglis and John MacIntyre coordinated, edited, prodded and encouraged its creation. It was a project that has taught us all a tremendous amount about Hamilton.

On a personal note, I offer my sincere apologies to my family and friends, who have been subjected to almost unending shouts of "Did you know….?" as we've driven through the city in recent months. I offer equally sincere thanks to Bill Freeman, who authored the fabulous "Hamilton — A People's History," which I've now almost completely memorized. Gratitude also goes out to the many Hamiltonians who contributed their thoughts and experiences to help create many illuminating Take 5 lists.

On behalf of us all — enjoy!

— Kim Arnott, September 2008

Table of Contents

12,000 Years Ago to Present . . . A Land Reunion . . . Desjardins
Canal Disaster . . . Robin McKee's Historic Hamilton Locations . . .
George and the Gore . . . Margaret Houghton's Turning Points in
Hamilton History . . .

From Nicknames to Population Booms . . . Ken Roberts' Five Essential
Hamilton Reads . . . You Know You're From Hamilton When . . .
Thomas McQuesten . . . Mayor Fred Eisenberger's Favourite Things
About Hamilton . . . Ben Zambiasi's Worst Things About Being a
Retired Ti-Cat Linebacker . . . Higher Ed . . .

From Aerotropolis and the Brow to the Scottish Rite and Tabbies, We
Give You the Lowdown on Hamilton Slang . . . Poet John Terpstra's
Hamilton Words . . . Steel Town Terms . . .

From the Mountain to Lake Ontario . . . Donna Reid's Five Hamilton
Buildings. . .Three Wrong Make a Right . . . Ryan McGreal's Top
Outdoor Fun . . . Paradise . . . The Five-Step Program . . . Staring at
the Devil . . . Trees and More Trees . . . Battlefield Park . . . Catherine
Gibbon's Favourite Landscapes . . . Royal Botanical Gardens . . . Jim
Heslop's Great Birdwatching Sites . . . Waterfalls . . .

Matt Hayes On Weather . . . Coldest, Hottest . . . Activities in Season
. . . Hurricane Hazel . . . Kathy Renwald's Garden Walks . . . The
Growing Season . . . Pass the Shovel . . .Blackout . . . Five Hamilton
Storms . . . Quake, Rattle and Roll . . . Winterfest . . .

"The Woman in Black" is a poem about one of Hamilton's most famous ghosts. It was written by Alexander Wingfield in 1873. She is rumoured to still live at the old Custom House and is still waiting for her sailor lover to come for her.

The Woman in Black

The ghosts - long ago - used to dress in pure white,
Now they're got on a different track,
For the Hamilton Ghost seems to take a delight
To stroll 'round the city in black.

Pat Duffy, who saw her in Corktown last night,
Has been heard to-day telling his friend
That she stood seven feet and nine inches in height,
And wore a large Grecian Bend.

A "Peeler," who met her, turned blue with affright,
And in terror he clung to a post;
His hair (once a carroty red) has turned white,
Since the moment he looked on the ghost.

Her appearance was frightful to gaze on, he said,
It filled him with horror complete;
For she looked unlike anything, living or dead,
That ever he'd seen on his beat.

Her breath seemed as hot as a furnace; besides,
It smelt strongly of sulphur and gin,
Two horns (a yard long) stuck straight out of her head,
And her hoofs made great clatter and din.

Her air was majestic, and terribly grand,
As she passed, muffled up in her veil;
A bottle of "ruin" she held in each hand,
And she uttered a low, plaintive wail;

"'There is rest for the weary,' but no rest for me;
I cannot find rest if I try,-
Three months and three days I have been on the spree;
(Mr. Mueller, 'How's that for high?')

"I have mixed in the world, both with 'spirits' and men,-
Once more with the spirits I'll go."
She stopped, took a sniff of the "ruin," and then
She popped into a cellar below.

He could hear her again, crying out from her den –
"To-night you will see me no more;
But I'll meet with you Saturday evening at ten,
By the fountain that stands in the Gore."

Some people that passed there this morning at two,
Found the "Peeler" still glued to his post;
He told them this yarn I have been telling you –
And that's the last news from the Ghost!

Hamilton:

A Timeline

12,000 years ago: The last glaciers retreat from the area now known as Hamilton. Lake Iroquois retreats and leaves what is now Lake Ontario.

6,000 years ago: Humans now inhabit the area, and the mastodon becomes extinct.

Around 1600: Attiwandaronk, or Neutral Indians, are living in the Hamilton area.

1616: French *coureur de bois* Etienne Brolé is the first white man to visit the Hamilton area.

1669: Hoping to find a route to the Pacific, La Salle and a group of companions land in Hamilton Harbour, approximately where La Salle Park now is.

1784: Land at the head of Lake Ontario is purchased from Mississaugas (a subtribe of the Anishinaabe First Nations people) by British.

1785: Loyalists begin settling Head-of-the-Lake.

1788: Townships at the Head-of-the-Lake are first surveyed.

1790: Richard Beasley, entrepreneur, land speculator, fur trader, politician and militia officer, settles at Burlington Heights, the present day site of Dundurn Castle.

1791: 31 families are recorded as living at the Head-of-the-Lake.

1792: Lake Geneva is renamed Burlington Bay.

1801: Mary Osborne of Saltfleet Township, east of Hamilton, hangs with her lover for the murder of her husband, Bartholomew London. This is the first documented murder in Hamilton and the first execution of a woman in Upper Canada.

1813: American schooners *Hamilton* and *Scourge* are sunk in a sudden storm on Lake Ontario.

1813: Following intense overnight fighting, British-Canadian forces win the Battle of Stoney Creek.

1814: "The Bloody Assize," a show trial held in Ancaster, convicts 15 men of high treason. Eight are subsequently executed.

1815: George Hamilton lays out streets for a town site in Barton Township, beginning the development of the city named in his honour.

1823: Approval is granted for reconstruction of a canal through the sand strip between Burlington Bay and Lake Ontario.

1826: Upper Canada's first paper mill is established at James Crooks on Spencer Creek, just west of Greensville.

1832: The Burlington Canal opens.

1835: Allan Napier MacNab completes Dundurn Castle, a stately Italianate villa, on land purchased from Richard Beasley.

1835: Gore Bank of Hamilton, Hamilton's first bank, is chartered. One of the town's earliest newspapers, The *Hamilton Gazette and General Advertiser*, begins publishing.

1837: Desjardins Canal opens, linking Dundas to shipping routes on Lake Ontario.

The Land Legend

Robert Land was one of the first white settlers in the Hamilton area. Fighting for the British against the Americans, he barely escaped execution in Pennsylvania. What he believed was that his wife and nine kids were not so lucky.

Truth of the matter was that his wife Phebe had escaped to Nova Scotia with the children, believing he had been killed. From Nova Scotia she moved to the Niagara area to collect on a land grant offered to those who stayed loyal to the British Crown. On her way to Niagara, she heard rumours of a man named Land living in what is now Hamilton.

She decided to check it out and hired a boat to take her there. It was not a rumour. The couple happily reunited, and took advantage of a land grant of 1,000 acres in what is now Hamilton. They helped build up the community and upon their deaths were buried in the Land Vault in historic Hamilton Cemetery.

1837: Allan MacNab leads troops to put down the Rebellion of 1837, for which he is knighted the following year.

1846: Hamilton receives its city charter; the first telegraph wire in Canada connects Hamilton and Toronto; and the *Hamilton Spectator* begins publishing.

1847: Thomas C. Watkins opens a store on James Street which evolves into the Right House, the first large department store in Hamilton.

1847: The Canada Life Assurance Company, Canada's first life insurance company, is opened by Hugh Cossart Baker, Jr.

1854: Great Western Railway opens in Hamilton, linking the city to lucrative U.S. markets via the Niagara Suspension Bridge.

1856: The first Canadian-built locomotives are constructed at a shop owned by Daniel C. Gunn, located on Wellington Street North.

1857: Desjardins Canal disaster; nearly sixty people are killed when a Great Western Railway train from Toronto to Hamilton crashes through a swing bridge over the canal.

1858: *Hamilton Times* begins publication.

1860: Edward, Prince of Wales, (the future King Edward VII) visits Hamilton.

1860: The Royal Hamilton Yacht Club is founded.

1872: Hamilton trade unionists emerge as the leaders of the Nine-Hour Movement, lobbying for a nine-hour workday and better working conditions.

The Desjardins Canal Disaster

Around 4:10 in the afternoon of March 12, 1857, the steam locomotive *Oxford* pulled out of Toronto on a routine trip to Hamilton. Canada had entered the railway age, with miles of tracks being laid down across the country almost as quickly as the locomotives that sped across them. But many of those who financed the projects were greedy, cutting corners and ignoring safety in the interest of profit.

As the train approached Hamilton and the junction with the main line of the Great Western Railway, the front axle of the locomotive broke. The train hurtled on towards the wooden swing bridge over the Desjardins Canal, near Dundas, just west of Hamilton.

Then the locomotive jumped the tracks, plunging sixty feet into the icy waters of the canal.

A woman living nearby happened to be looking out her window as the train crossed the bridge, shuddered, then disappeared. She hurried to the scene, slipping down the icy embankment to the water, where she found an 8-year-old girl, floating precariously on a cake of ice.

"Oh, don't mind me, save my brother," the girl said as the woman reached her. Nearby, a nine-year-old boy struggled to keep his head above water. Both children survived, as did their uncle, Owen Doyle, but their parents and other relatives died in the disaster. Rescuers worked by torchlight to rescue survivors and retrieve the dead, who were laid out in a shed close to the railway station, pending identification by relatives. In all, 59 perished. Twenty survived, many of them badly injured.

The inquest into the tragedy concluded that the bridge over the canal was "unsound, impaired and dangerous," and recommended that the Great Western Railway build an iron bridge.

13

1872: The Bank of Hamilton is established. In 1924, it merges with the forerunner of the Canadian Imperial Bank of Commerce.

1873: Hamilton Football Club plays its first game against the Toronto Argonauts and loses. Because of their yellow and black uniform, the Hamilton players are dubbed the Tigers in newspaper reports of the game.

1877: Hugh Cossart Baker, Jr. establishes the first commercial telephone service in Canada, in Hamilton.

1877: The Southam newspaper chain begins with the sale of the *Hamilton Spectator* by founder Robert Smiley to William Southam.

1878: First telephone exchange in the British Empire happens in Hamilton.

1882: E.D. Smith founds a company to market his fruit, eventually developing a famous line of preserves and jams.

1888: Because of its foundries and heavy industry, Hamilton is christened the "Birmingham of Canada" by visiting English businessmen.

1890: Hamilton's first public bowling alley and first public library open.

1892: The first electric streetcar begins operating in Hamilton, with two routes, one along King Street East and the other along James Street North.

1892: Toronto, Hamilton and Buffalo Railway begins running.

1893: Right House, the city's first large department store, officially opens.

Take 5 ROBIN MCKEE'S FIVE
HISTORIC HAMILTON LOCATIONS

Robin McKee is a researcher, writer and photographer. Through his business, Historical Perceptions, he offers historical walking and cemetery tours.

1. **Gore Park:** The original town square (even though it's triangular) is the location of the Gore Park fountain, a statue of Queen Victoria and a statue of Canada's first Prime Minister, Sir John A. Macdonald. Every year on Macdonald's birthday, a wreath is laid at the base of the monument.

2. **James Street South:** Between Gore Park and the Mountain are traces of the historical financial district, early churches, train stations and stately homes. Stairs lead to the top of the escarpment where Mountain Park offers a spectacular view of the city, including Burlington Heights, the Hamilton Beach Lighthouse and the Pumphouse and Waterworks.

3. **Burlington Heights:** Clustered around another spectacular high spot are Dundurn Castle, the Italianate villa built by Sir Allan Napier MacNab in 1832 and Hamilton cemetery, final resting place of many early settlers and prominent Hamiltonians.

4. **Beach Strip:** A historic mid-19th century lighthouse and lighthouse keeper's cottage guard the entrance to Hamilton Harbour. Nearby is the lift bridge, which was the main thoroughfare across the Burlington ship canal until the Skyway Bridge was completed in 1958. Picturesque older houses line the Beach Strip recalling the times when the area was a favourite destination for people trying to escape the summer heat.

5. **Hamilton Museum of Steam and Technology:** Cholera epidemics in the 1850s inspired Hamilton's city fathers to install the most modern waterworks available and bring clean water to city residents. Completed in 1859, the steam-operated waterworks are now a National Historic Site and the last functioning mid-Victorian era steam waterworks in North America.

1894: Billy Carroll, owner of the *Hamilton Herald*, starts the Around the Bay Road Race, now considered the oldest long-distance foot race in North America.

1897: Educator and reformer Adelaide Hoodless inspires Janet and Erland Lee to establish the first Women's Institute, a society aimed at improving homemaking and childcare.

1897: The Westinghouse Electric Company opens its Hamilton operation, the first branch outside the U.S.

1903: The first automobile club in Canada opens in Hamilton, aptly named the Hamilton Automobile Club.

1906: Hamilton-born marathon runner William Sherring wins an Olympic gold medal at the 1906 Athens games.

1906: The Hamilton Street Railway strike becomes violent, resulting in one of the few times the riot act is read in Hamilton.

1910: Steel Company of Canada (Stelco) is formed.

1912: Dominion Steel Casting Company, later known as Dofasco, opens in Hamilton.

1912: The Hamilton Alerts become the first Hamilton team to play in the Grey Cup. They beat the Toronto Argonauts 11 to 4.

1913: Battlefield Monument, commemorating the Battle of Stoney Creek during the War of 1812, is unveiled.

1914: The first concrete highway in Canada links Toronto and Hamilton.

George Hamilton and the Gore

Hamilton was named for George Hamilton, born in either 1787 or 1788, whose family belonged to a network of prosperous merchants in the Niagara area and in other parts of southern Ontario. When his Queenston property was burned during the War of 1812, he relocated to Head-of-the-Lake, an important military centre during the war.

Aware that there was talk of creating a new administrative district in the area, Hamilton purchased 257 lots in Barton Township, close to the proposed location of the district town.

His gamble paid off, to some extent, and he laid out the streets of the new community in the grid pattern that was typical of Upper Canada. Trouble was, the natural growth of the town was north of Hamilton's lands, towards the shores of Lake Ontario. So Hamilton tried various schemes to bring development southward. One strategy was the creation of a town square by combining an odd, triangular-shaped plot or gore, with another triangular piece owned by Nathaniel Hughson.

Seemed like a good idea until Hughson backed out. The Gore became an unsightly, muddy garbage dump. Then, in 1833, the town council tried to expropriate it. Hamilton sued, and won.

Three years later, George Hamilton died. For nearly a quarter century, nothing was done with the Gore. Hamilton council tried to make a deal with later owners and sell building lots there at least twice in the 1840s and 1850s, but these plans raised such a public outcry that they backed off.

Finally, in 1860, in an effort to beautify the town in time for the royal visit of the Prince of Wales, public money and private donations funded the creation of a park, complete with a three-tiered water fountain and trees.

Soon afterwards, vandals destroyed the trees and city fathers opted to lock the park up. It was not until June 1883 that Gore Park was formally opened to the public.

1914: Art Gallery of Hamilton opens in the old public library building located at 22 Main Street.

Take 5 MARGARET HOUGHTON'S FIVE
TURNING POINTS IN HAMILTON HISTORY

Margaret Houghton is the archivist in the Local History and Archives section of the Hamilton Public Library. She has written or edited several books, including *Hamilton Street Names: An Illustrated History* and *The Hamiltonians: 100 Fascinating Lives*.

1. **1785: First white settlers arrive at the Head-of-the-Lake.** Most were United Empire Loyalists who had fled the United States around the time of the American Revolution. Townships in the area were not surveyed until a few years later, between 1788 and 1793, but that didn't stop men like John Depew and Richard Beasley from taking up land.

2. **1846: Hamilton is incorporated as a city**, thirteen years after incorporation as a town. During that period, the population jumped from about 1,000 to 6,832.

3. **1910: Steel Company of Canada is formed.** Stelco, as it was later known, was for many years the major employer in Hamilton and contributed to Steeltown's lunch-bucket, blue-collar image.

4. **1942: Royal Hamilton Light Infantry lands at Dieppe**, France on August 19. The invasion was a disaster — nearly 20 percent of the 4,963 Canadians involved were killed. The Royal Hamilton Light Infantry was particularly hard hit. Of 582 soldiers who landed on the beach, 197 were killed and another 174 taken prisoner. Just over 100 men — fewer than one in five — escaped without any physical injury.

5. **2001: The new City of Hamilton is formed** with the amalgamation of Ancaster, Dundas, Flamborough, Glanbrook, Hamilton and Stoney Creek.

1915: Procter & Gamble Manufacturing Company officially opens its Hamilton facility, the first branch outside the U.S.

1921: With a population of 114,000, Hamilton is Canada's fifth-largest city. It also boasts the largest theatre in Canada, Pantages on King Street, with a capacity of 3,500.

1922: Hamilton's first radio station begins broadcasting. CKOC is the second station in Canada and the first in Ontario.

1923: Hamilton's Westinghouse plant becomes the first company in Canada to produce radios.

1925: Canada's first traffic lights turn on at the Delta.

1927: CHML, Hamilton's second radio station, goes on air.

1927: The first bag of airmail reaches Hamilton.

1928: Twenty-year-old Eileen Vollick becomes the first woman in Canada to hold a private pilot's license.

1929: Unveiling of the United Empire Loyalists statue outside the Wentworth County Courthouse. The statue is a Hamilton landmark.

1929: Hamilton's first skyscraper is built. The Piggott Building stands 64 m high, and costs about one million dollars.

1930: The first British Empire Games (later the Commonwealth Games) are held in Hamilton.

1930: McMaster University, established in 1887 in Toronto, moves to Hamilton.

1931: Mary Chambers Hawkins and other prominent Hamilton women open Canada's first birth control clinic.

1932: Ray Lewis of Hamilton becomes the first Canadian-born black to win an Olympic medal. Lewis receives a bronze for track and field in Los Angeles.

1934: Walker Anderson opens the first Canadian Tire associate store (franchise) on King Street, Hamilton.

1939: King George VI and Queen Elizabeth visit Hamilton.

1941: The province of Ontario establishes the Royal Botanical Gardens as an independent organization. The City of Hamilton started the gardens to beautify the northwest entrance to the community in the 1920s.

1943: Hamilton-born Jackie Callura defeats Jackie Wilson to become the world featherweight boxing champion.

1946: First drive-in theatre in Canada, the Skyway Drive-In, opens on Highway 8 near Gray's Road, Stoney Creek.

1946: United Steelworkers Local 1005 goes on strike against Stelco. The famous walkout forces employers to honour collective bargaining and inspires a resurgence of the labour movement in Canada.

1948: Surrounded by a crowd of admiring employees and reporters, a blue Champion sedan — the first in the city — rolls off the Studebaker assembly line.

1948: Canadian Westinghouse builds the first television set in Canada at its Hamilton plant.

1950: The amalgamation of the city's two football clubs, the Tigers and Wildcats, create the Hamilton Tiger-Cats.

1951: Princess Elizabeth — future Queen Elizabeth II — visits Hamilton for the first time.

1951: Hamilton Street Railways halts streetcar service.

1954: Hurricane Hazel hits Hamilton with heavy rains resulting in major flooding on October 15 and 16.

1954: CHCH becomes the first private television station to broadcast in Hamilton.

1955: The Centre Mall, Canada's first shopping mall and one of the first in North America, opens on Barton Street.

1956: Pioneer Gas, now one of the largest independent gas retailers in Canada, opens a station on Upper James Street.

1958: Burlington Bay Skyway opens. It is later expanded and renamed the Burlington Bay James N. Allan Skyway.

1960: The new City Hall opens on Main Street West.

1963: New Hamilton seal is adopted. Based on an 1847 design by Edward Acraman, the new seal conforms more closely to heraldic standards.

1964: First Tim Hortons coffee shop in Canada opens on Ottawa Street.

1966: Mohawk College grants its first diplomas. It has since grown into one of the largest provincially funded colleges in the province.

1968: Hamilton's Lincoln Alexander is elected to the House of Commons, becoming Canada's first black Member of Parliament.

1972: Canadian Football Hall of Fame opens.

1973: Birks Building at the corner of King and James is demolished to make way for a new law office. Oscar Wilde once called it "the most beautiful building in all of North America."

1974: Regional Municipality of Hamilton-Wentworth is inaugurated.

1981: Hamilton Convention Centre opens.

1983: Right House department store closes.

1985: Musician and U2 producer Daniel Lanois opens Grant Avenue Studios in Hamilton.

1985: Copps Coliseum opens.

1987: Team Canada, including Wayne Gretzky and Mario Lemieux, defeat Russian hockey team at Copps Coliseum to win the Canada Cup two games to one. All three games end in 6-5 scores.

1990: Over 14,000 Hamilton hockey fans plunk down non-refundable down payments for season tickets in anticipation of landing an NHL franchise. The Toronto Maple Leafs and the Buffalo Sabres unfortunately block the effort.

1993: Opening of Pier 4 and Harbourfront Park.

1994: Hamilton's Kresge store — the last of the Canadian chain — closes.

1995: Juno Awards are held in Hamilton for the first time. Hosts at the Copps Coliseum include Rick Mercer and Mary Walsh of *This Hour Has 22 Minutes*.

1997: Lincoln M. Alexander Parkway opens. Called the Linc by locals, the expressway is named in honor of former MP and Lieutenant-Governor of Canada, Lincoln Alexander, who never even had a driver's license.

1999: A part of Albert Einstein's brain is acquired by McMaster University for research purposes.

2001: Amalgamation forms the new city of Hamilton: Hamilton, Ancaster, Dundas, Flamborough, Glanbrook, and Stoney Creek.

2003: Businessman Michael DeGroote donates $10 million to upgrade the medical school at McMaster University. It is the largest single cash donation in Canadian history.

2003: Hamilton hosts the World Cycling Championships. This is the first time the races are held in Canada and only the second time ever outside Europe.

2006: Hamilton is ranked as the busiest of all Canadian Great Lake ports.

2007: Red Hill Creek Expressway opens in Hamilton. Construction is controversial because of the route through environmentally sensitive areas.

2008: Centre Mall closes pending a $100 million redevelopment with up to 65,000 m^2 of retail space. It will be the largest redevelopment project in east-end Hamilton's history.

Hamilton Essentials

Location: The city of Hamilton is strategically situated at the western tip of Lake Ontario midway between Toronto and Niagara Falls. The original settlement formed between the lake and the Niagara Escarpment, which rises up to a height of 335 metres. The rock face proved a challenge to expansion but accesses were cut in the rock so that roads could carry people to the top. As the city began to expand, more development took place on what the locals refer to as Hamilton Mountain. The city of Burlington borders Hamilton on the west, Grimsby on the east and travelling south of the city towards Lake Erie is one of Canada's largest First Nations Reservations — and home to the Six Nations.

Origin of the Name: Hamilton is named for George Hamilton (1788-1836), a wealthy merchant and politician who purchased 257 acres of land in Barton Township from James Durand in January 1815. Hamilton and Nathaniel Hughson, who was a property owner in the area as well, collaborated to prepare a proposal for a courthouse and jail on Hamilton's land. Hamilton then offered a large parcel of that land to the crown for the future site.

Date of Incorporation: Hamilton was incorporated as a town in 1833, and as a city in 1846. As it expanded, it annexed portions of Ancaster Township to the west, portions of Saltfleet Township to the east and portions of Barton Township to the east and south, eventually annexing all of Barton Township by 1960. When Regional Government was implemented in 1974, the city of Hamilton became part of the Regional Municipality of Hamilton-Wentworth. In 2001, it became the amalgamated city of Hamilton.

Motto: Together Aspire — Together Achieve

Nickname: The Hammer, Tiger Town and Steeltown

Coat of Arms: Created in 2001 for the amalgamation of the city of Hamilton with the city of Stoney Creek and the towns of Ancaster, Dundas, Flamborough, and Glanbrook.

City Flag: The city flag was designed by Bishop Spence, Canada's leading specialist in the Science of Flags or Vexillology, and granted to the city on July 15, 2003. The flag is divided with a Canadian Pale in royal blue with borders of golden yellow. The flag uses two major elements taken directly from the city's Grant of Arms. The golden yellow Cinquefoil is a heraldic flower of five petals that is the badge of the Clan Hamilton and represents the name of the city. The links circling the Cinquefoil, also golden yellow in colour, have two meanings — first, a circle of links is the standard heraldic symbol for unity, and second, they symbolize steel. The six larger links are symbolic of the six communities joined in unity.

Flower: Chrysanthemum

Time Zone: Eastern

Area Code(s): 905 and 289

Postal Code Span: L8E to L9H

System of Measurement: Metric

Driving Age: 16

Voting Age: 18

Drinking Age: 19

Statutory Holidays: New Years Day (January 1), Family Day (3rd Monday of February), Good Friday (the first Friday before Easter Sunday), Victoria Day (the first Monday before May 24), Canada Day (July 1), Civic Holiday (the first Monday in August), Labour Day (the first Monday in September), Thanksgiving (the second Monday in October), and Christmas Day (December 25).

Sister Cities: Shawinigan, Quebec; Mangalore, India; Fukuyama, Japan; Racalmuto, Italy; Flint, Michigan; Ma'Anshan, China; Abruzzo, Italy; Sarasota, Florida and Monterrey, Mexico.

Did you know...

that McMaster University alumni include two Nobel Prize winners — Dr. Myron Scholes and Bertram Brockhouse? Other grads include Roberta Bondar, Tommy Douglas (the father of Canadian Medicare and grandfather of Keifer Sutherland), Dalton McGuinty, Russ Jackson and Ivan Reitman.

They Said It

"It's a blend of professional and working class ... I like to have the plumber sitting beside the professor and both laughing at different things in the same joke."

– Comic Ron James said of his joy in performing in Hamilton.

POPULATION

The current population of the city of Hamilton is 692,911, up from 662,401 in 2001. This makes Hamilton the ninth most populous city in the country and the third largest city in the province. The population of all of Ontario in 2006 stood at 12,160,282. Hamilton's population was a little over 4 percent of the total Ontario population. In comparison, the population of Toronto, just 80 km away, was 2,503,281 and the population of Ottawa, the national capital, was 812,129.

According to studies carried out by the city of Hamilton, the population is expected to increase by approximately 81,000 households by 2031. The existing land area of the city will accommodate approximately 40,000 new dwellings.

POPULATION DENSITY (PEOPLE/KM^2)
Hamilton: 451.6
Toronto: 3,972
Tokyo: 5,751
New York City: 10,194
Alberta: 5.1
Ontario: 13.9

Did you know...

that Hamilton's population has increased by over 100,000 people since 1976?

POPULATION IN PERSPECTIVE (GMA)

Toronto: 5,597,000

Vancouver: 2,187,721

Ottawa: 1,302,055

Calgary: 1,079,310

Hamilton: 692,911

Source: Statistics Canada.

Take 5 KEN ROBERTS' FIVE ESSENTIAL
BOOKS ABOUT HAMILTON

Ken Roberts is chief librarian for the Hamilton Public Library. In addition to heading up the Hamilton Library system, Roberts is the newly elected president of the Canadian Library Association. The Hamilton library system was a co-recipient of the 2002 Ontario Library Association's President's Exceptional Achievement Award and Roberts himself won the 2001 Canadian Association of Public Libraries Outstanding Service Award.

1. *The Dictionary of Hamilton Biography Volume 1-4* (1981-1999) is the only biographical dictionary for a city in Canada. It documents not only the famous citizens but also the infamous and ordinary.

2. *A Mountain and a City: the story of Hamilton* by Marjorie Freeman Campbell (1966) was the first comprehensive history of the city written. There were other books about Hamilton written previously but they were not this extensive.

3. *Hamilton: A People's History* by Bill Freeman (2001) is the most recent comprehensive history of the city. It was a companion piece to the first video history of Hamilton [*Hamilton's history: where the rubber meets the road.*]

4. *The Head-of-the-Lake: a history of Wentworth County* by Charles M. Johnston (1967) is the only comprehensive history of the county of Wentworth.

5. *Hamilton at war: on the home front* by Margaret Houghton (2005) is a unique perspective on a Canadian city during a definitive period in our history.

YOU KNOW YOU'RE FROM

- You can get to an address downtown only making two right hand or two left hand turns.
- You love Hutch's fish and chips.
- At least once a summer you make the trek to Port Dover for Lake Erie perch.
- You know what the Jolley Cut is.
- "Large double-double to go, please" is your favourite phrase and everyone knows what to give you in return.
- You don't have to be religious to walk across the harbour.
- You think that "soot" and "rust" are normal colours for a car.
- You take vacations in New Jersey.
- You can find Clappison's Corner.
- You hate the Argos.
- You've climbed at least one set of stairs up the Mountain.
- If you're a smoker, you've bought at least one bag of reserve smokes.
- You dream of the day when the NHL will arrive.
- You used to hang out at the Chicken Roost.
- The sight of vacant stores is not unusual.
- You've been to a dance or a banquet at the Royal Connaught.
- You still call the airport Mount Hope.
- You've been to a lilac festival.
- You're fed up with all the plans for the Lister Block.
- You know what the Linc is.
- You're glad the Red Hill fight is over.
- You remember Tiny Talent Time.
- You know all about Plasinet.
- You've seen the CN Tower across the lake on a clear day.

HAMILTON WHEN . . .

- You know that two wrongs don't make a right but three lefts just might.
- You remember when the area code was 416.
- You object to being mistaken for someone from Burlington.
- You know that Mac is the university, not an apple or a computer.
- You call the Niagara Escarpment the Mountain.
- You have an Evelyn Dick story. Or know someone who knew her. Or actually knew her. Or really know what happened to her.
- You've fed pigeons in Gore Park.
- You've been stuck in traffic for an hour waiting for the lift bridge to come back down at the beach strip.
- You know what RBG, CCIW and HECFI stand for.
- You're completely confused by all the newly designated two-way streets.
- You don't want to check into the Barton Street Hilton.
- You know what follows "Oskee Wee Wee."
- You've lined up for Stoney Creek Dairy ice cream on the first sunny day in spring.
- You know that Copps Coliseum isn't named for Sheila.
- You've called the Roy Green show.
- You're still hanging on to that 1972 Grey Cup ticket stub.
- You've taken the bone-rattling ride across the city on the Beeline Express.
- You brag about having the first Tim Horton's store.
- You can look in 4 directions and still see a Tim Horton's each way.
- All the roads in "Hamilton" are plowed in the winter before any other township.
- You know who Bruiser is.

POPULATION BY AGE AND SEX

	Males	Females
0-14	46,155	43,740
15-24	35,145	34,140
25-44	67,090	69,850
45-64	65,095	67,960
65+	32,205	43,190

Source: Statistics Canada.

MEDIAN AGE
- Men 38.5
- Women 40.7

Take 5 MAYOR FRED EISENBERGER'S
FAVOURITE THINGS ABOUT HAMILTON

Mayor Eisenberger was born in Amsterdam in 1952 and immigrated to Canada, settling in Hamilton with his family when he was eight years old. Fred graduated with honours from Mohawk College in planning and community development, and has since taken courses towards his Bachelor of Environmental sciences at the University of Waterloo and political science at McMaster. He was first elected to Hamilton City Council as the representative for Ward 5 in 1991 and became mayor in his second attempt in 2006.

1. Webster's Falls.
2. The escarpment.
3. The fact that Hamilton is green and fully developed.
4. Future opportunities and the many possibilities that make it exciting to be in Hamilton.
5. The future of the city is bright and Hamilton is a "small big town" that is warm, welcoming and close. The community is very much connected.

LIFE EXPECTANCY

	Ontario	Canada
Males	75.9	75.4
Females	81.3	81.2

Source: Statistics Canada.

Bio THOMAS MCQUESTEN

If you love to scuffle through the autumn leaves in Gage Park, sniff the spring tulips in the Royal Botanical Gardens or watch the wild birds in Coote's Paradise, don't forget to offer thanks to Tom McQuesten. A successful Hamilton lawyer and politician, McQuesten's love for green spaces still blooms across the city's landscape today, more than 60 years after his death.

As a city councillor (1913-20) and member of Hamilton's Board of Parks Management (1922-48), he spearheaded the purchase and development of more than 2,500 acres of parkland in the Hamilton area, including Gage Park, Inch Park, Scott Park, Mountainside Park and Coote's Paradise.

In 1932, under McQuesten's greening influence, Hamilton boasted the largest acreage of developed parklands and playgrounds of any Canadian city. McQuesten, whose family's Jackson Street mansion Whitehern is now preserved as a historic museum, was also instrumental in bringing both McMaster University and the Royal Botanical Gardens to the city.

In 1934, he was elected to the provincial government and appointed Minister of Highways. In that role, he oversaw the construction of the Queen Elizabeth Highway, as well as many other Ontario highways and bridges. He also served as Chairman of the Niagara Parks Commission and oversaw the construction of the Niagara Parkway, the Floral Clock and the School for Apprentice Gardeners, which still provides training in park maintenance.

McQuesten was named Hamilton Citizen of the Year shortly before his death in 1948. The book *Green City: People, Nature & Urban Place*s is one of just 11 industrial cities that have managed to successfully co-exist with nature, something the author attributes directly to McQuesten.

CRADLE TO GRAVE
- Births (yearly) 6,227
- Deaths (yearly) 4,553

Source: Ontario Ministry of Government Services.

MARRIAGE
- Rate of marriage in Hamilton: 3.7 (per 1,000 population)
- Marriage rate in Nunavut, Canada's lowest: 2.3
- Marriage rate in Prince Edward Island, Canada's highest: 6.0
- National marriage rate: 4.7

Source: Statistics Canada.

Take 5 — BEN ZAMBIASI'S FIVE WORST THINGS
ABOUT BEING A RETIRED TI-CAT LINEBACKER

A star linebacker with the Hamilton Tiger-Cats from 1978 to 1987, Ben Zambiasi was inducted into the Canadian Football Hall of Fame in 2004. He lives in Hamilton with his wife and daughter, and hates having to watch football games from the Ivor Wynne stands rather than the sidelines.

1. People coming up to me and saying, "Wow! I always thought you were so much bigger!"
2. Being an armchair quarterback instead of trying to rip the quarterback's arm off.
3. Longing for the days when I had to eat four meals just to maintain my weight.
4. Learning that tackling the competition and knocking them on their butts is not considered a transferable job skill for most career choices.
5. Not seeing my teammates, who loved and understood the game as much as me. Thank goodness for alumni events.

Take 5 FIVE TOP TOURIST ACTIVITIES
FOR OVERNIGHT VISITORS

1. **Visiting Friends and Relatives**
2. **Shopping**
3. **Outdoor/Sports Activity**
4. **Sightseeing**
5. **Visiting Historic Sites**

Source: Tourism Hamilton.

FAMILY STRUCTURE

- Number of all families (married and common law, single parent): 195,905
- Percentage of married-couple families: 73
- Percentage of common-law-couple families: 10
- Percentage of male lone-parent families: 3
- Percentage of female lone-parent families: 14

Source: Statistics Canada.

URBAN / RURAL LAND AREA (PERCENTAGE)

Community	Urban	Rural
Ancaster	15	85
Dundas	47	53
Flamborough	2	98
Glanbrook	9	91
Hamilton	100	0
Stoney Creek	39	61

Did you know...

that Isabella Whyte, now resting in the Hamilton Cemetery, is rumoured to have been Queen Victoria's half-sister?

Take 5 FIVE HAMILTON FIRSTS

1. The first telephone exchange in the British Commonwealth happened in Hamilton in 1878.
2. The first matches in the country were made by the Green family in the early 1830s.
3. Lifesavers (candies) were invented by the Beechnut Company of Hamilton in 1933.
4. Westinghouse in Hamilton was the first company in Canada to manufacture radios (1923) and electric air cleaners (1944).
5. Hamiltonians Solomon Robinson, John Robinson and John Lewison produced the first ice cream cones in Canada at their King Street plant in 1908.

URBAN / RURAL POPULATION (PERCENTAGE)

Community	Urban	Rural
Ancaster	78	22
Dundas	94	6
Flamborough	36	64
Glanbrook	28	72
Hamilton	100	0
Stoney Creek	92	8

Source: City of Hamilton.

They Said It

"Sure, the Hammer has its warts but we've got rings around our fingers for the city of Hamilton."

– Songwriter Kathleen Edwards, who recently moved to the city and is married to Hamiltonian guitarist Colin Cripps.

VISIBLE MINORITIES

Not a visible minority	86.4 percent
South Asian	3.0 percent
Black	2.8 percent
Chinese	1.9 percent
Southeast Asian	1.2 percent
Latin American	1.1 percent
Arab	1.1 percent
Filipino	0.8 percent
West Asian	0.7 percent
Multiple	0.4 percent
Korean	0.3 percent
Other	0.2 percent
Japanese	0.2 percent

Source: Statistics Canada.

RELIGIOUS AFFILIATION (PERCENTAGE)

Protestant: 34
Catholic: 37
Other Christian: 3
Christian Orthodox: 3
Buddhist: 1
Muslim: 2
Hindu: 1
Jewish: 1
Other religions: >1
None: 18

Source: Statistics Canada.

Did you know...

that Columbia International College is the largest private boarding university-preparatory school in Canada with students from 51 different countries?

They Said It

"Hamilton in 50 years will be the forward cleat in a 'golden horseshoe' of industrial development from Oshawa to the Niagara River... 150 miles long and 50 miles wide... It will run from Niagara Falls on the south to about Oshawa on the north and take in numerous cities and towns already there, including Hamilton and Toronto."

– Westinghouse President Herbert H. Rogge in a 1954 speech to the Hamilton Chamber of Commerce.

LANGUAGE (SPOKEN MOST OFTEN AT HOME)

English: 88.7 percent
French: 0.4 percent
Non-official language: 10.9 percent

Source: Statistics Canada.

FULL-TIME STUDENTS ENROLLED

Universities and Colleges

- McMaster University: 21,286 full time, 3,835 part time and 5,336 summer sessions
- Redeemer University College: 849 full time
- Mohawk College: 10,000 full time, 47,000 part time and 3,000 apprentices
- Columbia International College: 1,300 foreign students

Schools

- Public schools: over 55,000 students enrolled in 60 schools
- Dundas Calvin School: 231 students
- Calvin Christian School: 420 students
- Hillfield Strathallan College: 1,100 students

They Said It

"Hamilton built Canada. Those who know a bit of history know Hamilton was the financial capital of Canada long before Bay St. in another city not far away. It had one of the first homes with electric lighting and an elevator. The list of firsts goes on and on."

– Jamie West, broadcaster.

HIGHER EDUCATION

McMaster University is named after Senator William McMaster (1811-1887), who bequeathed substantial funds to endow "a Christian school of learning." The university was incorporated under the terms of an act of the Legislative Assembly of Ontario in 1887. The new university, housed in McMaster Hall in Toronto, offered courses in arts and theology. Degree programs began in 1890, with degrees first being conferred in 1894.

In 1930, McMaster relocated to Hamilton and in 1957 the university became a non-denominational private institution. Today, more than 60 percent of the student body comes from outside Hamilton to study everything from arts and science to engineering to medicine to business and beyond. The university is the major knowledge generator in the city.

Redeemer University College is a small undergraduate liberal Christian arts and science school located in a rural section of Ancaster. It was originally founded in 1982 and until 2000 it was known as Redeemer College.

While Mohawk College's main campus is in Hamilton, the school has campuses in nearby Brantford and Stoney Creek. Mohawk grew out of what in 1947 became the Provincial Institute of Textiles, located at what is now the Wentworth Campus. It was one of the first Ontario schools to offer specialized post-secondary training in the technical fields. A decade later, it was renamed the Hamilton Institute of Technology.

Its main campus sits on 66 acres of land that originally grew food for the patients at the mental hospital across the road. The original root cellar for that farm forms part of the student centre known today as the Arnie. Today it is a leading college in engineering, applied arts and business, and health technology.

HEALTH CARE PROFESSIONALS
- Physicians: about 800
- Dentists: 359
- Nurses: 10,338 in the Local Health Integration Network that includes Hamilton
- Pharmacists: 370

CANADIAN COMMUNITY HEALTH SURVEY
(Percentage of respondents)

	Hamilton	Canada	Ontario
Overweight	55.5	48.5	49.2
Physically active	50.9	49.0	48.8
Has a regular Dr.	94.7	84.4	90.4
Regular smoker	24.4	21.9	20.6

Source: The Canadian Community Health Survey.

COMMUNICATIONS
Daily/weekly newspapers include the *Hamilton Spectator* daily newspaper plus *Hamilton Community News*, who publish the following weeklies; the *Dundas Star News, Ancaster News, Stoney Creek News* and the *Mountain News. View Magazine* is a weekly free paper with lists of groups playing at various clubs in the city, and *Hamilton Magazine* is a glossy magazine with features about the city.

Weblinks

City of Hamilton

www.myhamilton.ca

The main page to find out everything you need to know; services, departments, recreation, culture, public health, social services, projects, news, and business — just to name a few.

Hamilton Tourism

www.tourismhamilton.com

The official tourism site that will fill you in on tours, events, festivals, arts, shopping, campgrounds, attractions, and so much more.

The Hamilton Spectator

www.thespec.com

Hamilton's own daily newspaper; check it out online to keep up with the latest news.

Slang:

Aerotropolis: 1,100 acres of land clustered around the Hamilton airport slated for future employment lands development.

Ancaster: Found in the southwest corner of Hamilton, atop the escarpment, and considered the city's ritziest neighbourhood. Established in 1792, Ancaster was amalgamated with Hamilton in 2001.

Around the Bay: An annual 30 km race around Burlington Bay with bragging rights as the oldest road race in North America.

B-Line: The express bus that runs across the lower city.

Barton Street Hilton: Hamilton's jail, officially known as the Hamilton Wentworth Detention Centre.

Bay (the): A Hamiltonian using the phrase is more likely to be referring to the body of water (Burlington Bay) than the department store.

Beach Strip: The narrow strip of land separating Lake Ontario from Burlington Bay.

Brow (the): The edge of the Mountain.

Black 'n Gold: Nickname for the Hamilton Tiger-Cats, in reference to the team's colours.

Bruiser: The mascot for the Hamilton Bulldogs hockey team.

Canusa: Annual youth sporting competition between Hamilton and Flint, Michigan, now in its 51st year.

Catch (the): The game-tying touchdown catch made by Hamilton Tiger-Cat Tony Champion in the 1989 Grey Cup against the Saskatchewan Roughriders.

Centre (the): Once named the Greater Hamilton Shopping Centre, this east-end mall is now simply known as the Centre Mall.

Clappison's: Hwy 6 access up the Mountain toward Guelph. The intersection of Hwys 6 and 5 is known as Clappison's Corners.

Cootes: May refer to Cootes Paradise or adjacent Cootes Drive.

Copps: Victor K. Copps Coliseum, the downtown arena named after a long-time city mayor and father of federal politician Sheila Copps.

Delta (the): The east-end intersection where King and Main streets cross and become two-way roads.

Double-double: A coffee prepared with two cream and two sugar.

Dundas: A valley community nestled along the Niagara Escarpment in Hamilton's west-end. Amalgamated with the city of Hamilton in 2001.

EHR: East Hamilton Radio, an independent electronics store in east Hamilton.

Take 5 POET JOHN TERPSTRA'S FIVE
WORDS TO DESCRIBE HAMILTON

John Terpstra's most recent book is *Two or Three Guitars: Selected Poems*. An earlier work, *Disarmament*, was short-listed for the Governor Generals Award. His poetry has won the CBC Radio Literary Prize, the Bressani Prize, and several Arts Hamilton literary awards. He has written a creative non-fiction book about Hamilton, *Falling Into Place*; and his work, *The Boys, or Waiting for the Electricians Daughter*, a memoir, was short-listed for both the Charles Taylor Prize for non-fiction and the BC Award for Canadian non-fiction.

1. **Location** (Location, Location). Lying on a narrow swath of land between the Niagara Escarpment and Burlington Bay, at the western-most tip of the easternmost Great Lake: the centre of the universe.

2. **Industry.** We made things here, many things. Now we don't make so many. We are re-inventing ourselves.

3. **Underdog**. As Canada is to the U.S.; as the rest of the provinces are to Ontario; so is Hamilton to its next-door neighbour, Toronto. We know how the rest of the country feels.

4. **Waterfalls**. Seventy-five (and still counting) cascades of varying intensities fall over the edge and through gorges of the Niagara Escarpment as it winds its way through the city.

5. **Paradise**. Bury me in the ancient, glacial sand-and-gravel bar that also winds through the city, looking west over the water of Cootes Paradise.

Flamborough: A collection of 15 primarily rural communities atop the Niagara Escarpment, Flamborough was merged with the city of Hamilton in 2001.

Glanbrook: Taking in the towns of Binbrook and Mount Hope, Glanbrook encompasses much of the agricultural land in Hamilton. It was amalgamated with the city of Hamilton in 2001.

GO to TO: Riding the GO train or bus to Toronto.

Golden Horseshoe: The prosperous horseshoe-shaped strip of land running around Lake Ontario from Toronto to the American border. At the westernmost tip of the lake, Hamilton sits roughly at the centre of the horseshoe.

Hammer (the): Nickname for Hamilton.

Hess: Nickname for Hess Village, a popular collection of bars and nightclubs just west of downtown.

HSR: Hamilton Street Railway, the city's public transit system.

Labour Day Classic: The annual football match between century-old rivals, the Hamilton Tiger-Cats and the hated Toronto Argonauts.

Linc (the): Lincoln Alexander Parkway, named for the groundbreaking local politician, who ironically, never held a driver's license.

Lower City: The part of Hamilton below the escarpment.

Lunchbucket Head: A factory worker.

MAC: An affectionate nickname for McMaster University.

Marauders: The moniker for McMaster sports teams.

Meadowlands: Hamilton's first collection of big-box stores, located alongside the Linc in Ancaster.

Take 5 FIVE BASIC STEEL-MAKING TERMS

1. **Blast Furnace:** A towering cylinder lined with heat-resistant (refractory) bricks, used to smelt iron from iron ore. Its name comes from the "blast" of hot air and gases forced up through the iron ore, coke, and limestone that load the furnace.

2. **Coke:** The basic fuel consumed in blast furnaces in the smelting of iron. Coke is a processed form of coal. About 1,000 pounds of coke are needed to process a ton of pig iron.

3. **Ingot:** A form of semi-finished type of metal. Liquid metal is teemed (poured) into molds, where it slowly solidifies. Once the metal is solid, the mold is stripped, and the 25- to 30-ton ingots are then ready for subsequent rolling or forging.

4. **Pickling:** Process that cleans a steel coil of its rust, dirt and oil so that further work can be done to the metal. When hot-rolled coils cool, rust forms on the unprotected metal; often coils are stored or transported while exposed to outside air and water. Through a continuous process, the steel is uncoiled and sent through a series of hydrochloric acid baths that remove the oxides (rust). The steel sheet is then rinsed and dried.

5. **Pig Iron:** The name for the melted iron produced in a blast furnace, containing a large quantity of carbon (above 1.5 percent). Named long ago when molten iron was poured through a trench in the ground to flow into shallow earthen holes, the arrangement looked like newborn pigs suckling. The central channel became known as the "sow," and the molds were "pigs."

Source: Michelle Applebaum Research.

Mountain (the): Hamiltonian's grandiose name for the 90 m rise of rock known to the rest of the world as the Niagara Escarpment.

Never Win Stadium: A less-than-affectionate nickname for Ivor Wynne Stadium, used primarily during unsuccessful Hamilton Tiger-Cat seasons.

North End: One of the oldest areas in the city, wedged between downtown and Lake Ontario.

Oskee-Wee-Wee: The beginning of a Hamilton Tiger-Cats cheer, although often used on its own as an expression of enthusiasm for the team.

Rail Trail: Walking and cycling trails built on former railway corridors.

RBG: Acronym for Royal Botanical Gardens.

Red Hill: Red Hill Valley Parkway, whose name came from the creek and valley running down the Mountain to the lake.

Reserve Smokes: Cheap cigarettes purchased from stores on the Six Nations Reserve near Brantford.

Scottish Rite: The castle-like building at the corner of King and Queen Streets. Originally built in 1895 as a home for tobacco magnate George Tuckett, it now serves as a club for local Freemasons.

Skyway: Burlington Bay James N. Allan Skyway bridge, crossing Burlington Bay between Hamilton and Burlington.

Spec: *Hamilton Spectator*, the city's daily newspaper.

Steel City: Hamilton's nickname.

StreetBeat: A popular *Hamilton Spectator* column written by Paul Wilson.

Stoney Creek: The most eastern community in the city, Stoney Creek was amalgamated with Hamilton in 2001.

Tabbies: Nickname for the Hamilton Tiger-Cats, also frequently shortened to Ticats.

T.C.: veteran mascot for the Hamilton Tiger-Cats. Joined a few years ago by fellow mascot Stripes.

Upper City: The part of the city atop the Mountain. Street names mirror those in the lower city, but with Upper added in front.

Urban Geography

Present day Hamilton sits in an area referred to as the Niagara peninsula, which is that area that lies on the south shore of Lake Ontario. Indeed it is Hamilton Harbour on the shores of Lake Ontario that marks the northern limit of the city.

The other defining feature of the Hamilton landscape is the Niagara Escarpment or what is referred to locally as the Mountain. The escarpment, simply stated, is a ridge composed of rock strata with a long, gradual slope on one side and a relatively steep cliff on the other. The Niagara Escarpment dates back in geological history to some 430 to 450 million years ago when it laid under a shallow warm sea. As the seas receded, it left the massive escarpment that runs from Watertown, New York through Hamilton and beyond to Wisconsin. In the case of Hamilton it runs through the middle of the city, effectively dividing it into 'upper' and 'lower' parts, and giving it its definitive landscape.

The steep rock face of the Niagara Escarpment has provided the city with a backdrop that includes more than 60 waterfalls. It also forms the basis of many challenging hiking trails. The original settlers populated the area from the lake to the escarpment. As the city grew, settlement expanded up the "mountain" and gaining access became a challenge. Winter storms still pose a challenge.

LONGITUDE AND LATITUDE

On the global grid, Hamilton is located at latitude 43.97 N and longitude 78.10 W. This places it on similar latitude lines with cities such as Krasnodar, Russia; Nice, France and Rome, Italy and on near-par longitude with Guantanamo, Cuba; Guayaquil, Ecuador and Lima, Peru Panama.

LAND AREA

Hamilton is 1,117.2 km^2 in size, which is huge compared to Toronto's 630 km^2, Montreal's 365 km^2 and Vancouver's 115 km^2.

A UNITED NATIONS BIOSPHERE RESERVE

In 1990, UNESCO (the United Nations Educational, Scientific and Cultural Organization) named the Niagara Escarpment a World Biosphere Reserve, recognizing it as one of the world's unique natural wonders. In Canada, the Niagara Escarpment stretches 725 km from Queenston on the Niagara River to Tobermory at the tip of the Bruce Peninsula.

In Ontario, the escarpment contains more than 100 sites of geological significance including some of the best exposures of rocks and fossils of the Silurian and Ordovician Periods (405 to 500 million years old) to be found anywhere in the world.

The escarpment contains more than 300 bird species, 53 mammals, 36 reptiles and amphibians, 90 fish and 100 varieties of special interest flora including 37 types of wild orchids. The Hamilton area alone is home to 225 different species of birds that use the area for nesting and migration staging areas.

They Said It

> "I think we're really good at knocking down good old buildings in this town and not being accountable for it."
>
> **– Tom Wilson, rock musician.**

They Said It

"The most successful cities in the world all share two things: a great university and old architecture. Hamilton has both."

– Glen Murray, president of the Canadian Urban Institute and former Winnipeg mayor.

HAMILTON IS . . .

- 409 km from Ottawa
- 1,987 km from Halifax
- 4,479 km from Vancouver
- 3,433 km from Calgary
- 66 km from the United States border
- 567 km from New York City

HAMILTON BOASTS

- 3,080 km of roads
- 2,662 acres of parkland
- 20 arenas
- 13 sports and fitness facilities
- 35,000-seat Ivor Wynne Stadium
- 1,300 seat Bernie Arbour Stadium
- 19 community centres
- 67 cemeteries (55 of those abandoned)

Did you know...

that almost all of the water in the Great Lakes is of glacial origin?

Did you know...

that the rocks present in the escarpment consist of sandstone, limestone, shale and dolostone?

TRAFFIC SYSTEMS INVENTORY

- 492 traffic signals
- 35 pedestrian signals
- 49 km communication lines
- 36,000 standard street lights

Take 5 DONNA REID'S FIVE BUILDINGS
OF ARCHITECTURAL SIGNIFICANCE

Donna Reid is chair of the 2008 Hamilton Doors Open Program. The program seeks to celebrate, educate and inform citizens and visitors of the importance of the architectural, cultural and historical sites in Hamilton by allowing visitors free access to properties that are not usually open to the public, or would normally charge an entrance fee. In 2007, they opened 59 sites and entertained over 28,000 visits.

1. **270 Sherman St. N, formerly the Imperial Cotton Company Complex.** This was built in 1900 and designed by Edmund Patterson. It is an example of Hamilton's once flourishing textile industry and is currently being revitalized as a creative studio space for artists of all genres, including photography, print making, painting, music, mixed and multi media.

2. **Auchmar Manor and Estate** was built in 1855 and is the last surviving country estate on Hamilton Mountain. This Gothic Revival manor and its walled and landscaped grounds was built for the Honourable Isaac Buchanan — Scotsman, entrepreneur, civic leader, politician and legendary public figure in Canada. Auchmar is a significant cultural landscape under threat.

- 2,850 decorative lights
- 150,000 traffic control signs
- 100,000 other signs
- 3,000 km pavement markings

Source: City of Hamilton.

3. **Hamilton GO Centre and TH&B Railway Museum** was built between 1931 and 1933 and designed by Fellheimer & Wagner of New York. It is a rare example of an Art Moderne public building with curved forms, polished metals, and machined detailing throughout.

4. **Hamilton City Hall** is a building in the international style that elicits extreme reactions. I appreciate it because of its details — the cantilevered main staircase, the Murano glass tile mosaics that are a different colour on each floor, the brass bullet hinges on teak doors, and the unique aluminum inside staircase that runs from basement to rooftop, the domed skylight in the Council chambers and so much more.

5. **The Bank of Montreal.** It is a downtown landmark with strong neo classical lines. The detailed carvings are by William Oosterhoff, once the sculptor in residence at the Parliament Building in Ottawa. The massive banking hall, with its towering ionic columns, is a treat for the eyes. It has survived numerous threats of demolition and in 2005 was beautifully restored and adaptively re-used by a law firm.

Did you know...

that the tallest building in Hamilton is Century 21 Tower at 42 stories and about 450 feet high?

LAKE ONTARIO

Formed by water eroding bedrock and then shaped by glaciers, Lake Ontario took its present form about 11,000 years ago, and continues to move slowly southward. The name was applied to the lake as early as 1641, long before the province of Ontario came into being in 1867.

In prehistoric times, Lake Ontario marked the boundary that separated the Iroquois and Huron nations and was used as an important trade route by various First Nations peoples. European settlers were also drawn to its shores.

Lake Ontario is the 13th largest lake in the world, with an area of over 19,000 km^2 and an average depth of 86 m. Eighty percent of its water flows in from Lake Erie.

Today, approximately one in four Canadians live close to the lake. Ontario's "Golden Horseshoe" — the area encompassing Toronto, Hamilton and the Niagara peninsula — is the most heavily populated area of the country and an important farming and industrial region. Lakefront revitalization has been recognized as not only a vital component in Hamilton's economic life but environmental and cultural well-being as well.

The Hamilton Harbour area has become a tourist attraction, with 15.5 km of paved trails, a waterfront trolley and a sightseeing boat that offers a spectacular view of one of Canada's most stunning waterfronts.

Did you know...

that Hamilton has 76 different species of trees?

Take 5 RYAN MCGREAL'S TOP FIVE
OUTDOOR ACTIVITIES

Ryan McGreal is the editor of *Raise the Hammer*, a local web magazine focusing on urban revitalization and sustainability.

1. **Industrial Trail:** Hamilton is well-known for its industrial heritage. To this day, the steel industry still occupies a significant, if shrinking, place in the local economy. We have the Made in Hamilton Industrial Trail, a series of loops highlighting significant sites from Hamilton's 19th and 20th century history of industrial development.

2. **Waterfront:** Take the free trolley shuttle from downtown Hamilton to the waterfront and enjoy the beautifully restored Bayfront Park and boat launch. Bring a picnic lunch or stop in for a bite at William's Coffee Pub. From there, you can walk, cycle, inline skate or ride the Waterfront Trolley out to Princess Point to enjoy Cootes Paradise. Close the day with a Hamilton Harbour boat cruise.

3. **Confederation Park:** Head east to Confederation Park to enjoy a beautiful 3.5 km promenade, perfect for strolling, cycling or just enjoying the view. Be sure to stop in at Baranga's on the Beach, a Mediterranean restaurant on the historic Van Wagner's Beach Rd. This area also includes Wild Waterworks, an 83-hectare water park.

4. **Waterfalls:** Because it straddles the Niagara Escarpment, Hamilton enjoys (and occasionally suffers) a unique geography on two levels. The myriad rivers and streams running down from the Mountain have produced an abundance of waterfalls, some of them spectacular. Conservation Hamilton has produced a map of the 32 most prominent falls, any of which are worth a visit to enjoy some hiking and sightseeing.

5. **Bruce Trail:** The 800-km Bruce Trail starts in Niagara and runs all the way to Tobermory on the tip of the Bruce Peninsula. It passes through Hamilton along the Niagara Escarpment and offers excellent hiking, including several staircases joining the upper and lower city.

GETTING AROUND

It's been said that two wrongs don't make a right, but in Hamilton, three left-hand turns might accomplish the task. One-way streets have been a feature of the city since the 1950s, and while they might baffle the occasional visitor, they make east-west travel across the lower city quick and painless. In fact, thanks to the well-synchronized traffic lights along King and Main Streets, even the city's B-Line express bus can travel from

Paradise

Visitors to Hamilton who drive into the city from the east and from Toronto along Highway 403 have a spectacular view of paradise on the right hand side. Cootes Paradise is an 840-hectare wildlife sanctuary containing a 250-hectare coastal wetland; Cootes Paradise Marsh is considered one of the most important waterfowl staging habitats on the lower Great Lakes and the largest nursery habitat for fish in the region.

The area is named for Captain Thomas Cootes, a British officer stationed at Fort Niagara in 1700s, who is said to have returned to the area so often for duck hunting that it deserved his name. One of the most unique qualities of this area is its location so close to urban core. Many of the hiking trails around Cootes Paradise literally start a stone's throw from residential areas, bus stops, and a four-lane highway, Cootes Dr., that connects west Hamilton and Dundas to McMaster University.

The need to protect the marshland was officially recognized in 1927 when the area was given the designation of sanctuary. The designation, however, could not stem the effects of rapid growth and industrialization. The streams flowing into Cootes Paradise were contaminated, but the restoration of Cootes Paradise, led by the Royal Botanical Gardens, is now the largest fresh-water marsh restoration project of its kind in North America.

The bid to rid Cootes of carp received an added boost in December of 2007 when strong wind and low water levels in Lake Ontario chased just about all the carp out of Cootes. It was the first time Cootes had fully drained since 1965. Many beneficial species have slowly begun to return to the marsh. The RBG has begun an aggressive planting program, proving you really can rebuild Paradise.

McMaster University to Eastgate Square in about 30 minutes.

While the one-way system is speedy, it isn't universally popular. Critics have argued that five lanes of fast-moving traffic add little to the streetscape and make downtown renewal more challenging. In 2005, two-way traffic was introduced to the key north-south downtown streets of James and John. Debate about converting King and Main Streets to two-way traffic continues.

For those looking to leave the lower city and climb the Mountain, one of the biggest challenges is figuring out where you'll end up. While nine access routes (Jolley Cut, Kenilworth, Sherman, Queen Street (also known as Beckett's Drive), Hwy 403, Mount Albion Road, Hwy 20, James Street and Claremont) take drivers up the escarpment, they all must cross the Mountain face to maintain a reasonable grade. That means that the Kenilworth Access doesn't take you to Upper Kenilworth, but rather, to Upper Ottawa. Likewise, the James Street Access dumps drivers out onto West Fifth Street, not Upper James.

The city's routes up the Mountain were highlighted in 2003 when the World Road Cycling Championship came to Hamilton. With millions of television viewers around the world watching, the bike racers pedaled up Beckett's Drive, and up and down the James Street and Claremont accesses. The race was held in Hamilton because of the challenge the Niagara Escarpment provided for racers.

Travellers looking to avoid Hamilton altogether can now do that as well, thanks to the 2007 completion of the Red Hill Valley Parkway. After decades of debate, the highly-controversial expressway finally opened, joining up with the Lincoln Alexander Parkway to create a high-speed connection between Hwy 403 and the QEW.

Did you know...

that Peregrine Falcons were spotted in Hamilton in 1995 and it was discovered that a pair of them nest high up on a ledge of the downtown Sheraton Hotel? Volunteers keep watch over them and a number of eggs have hatched over the years.

PARK IT!

The city of Hamilton boasts over 3,100 acres of parkland at 457 locations, over 49 km of city-owned trails, and in excess of 1,690 acres of open space property at 52 locations, offering many opportunities for people of all ages to get outdoors and explore nature.

The many recreational trails encourage hikers, cyclists, rollerbladers, and nature lovers to enjoy the natural landscapes of the

Take 5 THE HAMILTON
FIVE-STEP PROGRAM

In addition to vehicular access up the escarpment, the city has put in five sets of stairs for those ambitious types who want to exercise. The local paper has taken to calling it the Steeltown Stomp.

1. **The Chedoke Stairs** that run from the municipal Chedoke Golf Club to Scenic Dr. are made of 289 steps. No one knows when they were built.

2. **The Dundurn Stairs** go from Dundurn St. to Becket Dr, and are made of 326 steps. The original wooden steps were replaced with steel steps in the 1990s.

3. **The James St. Stairs** start near St. Joseph's Hospital and comprise of 227 steps; they take people to the top of the Claremont Access. A photo exists of these stairs taken around 1860. The steps were replaced in 1987.

4. **The Wentworth Stairs** now number 498 and are still the longest. Originally, there were 570 wooden stairs built in 1903, but in 1983 they were destroyed by a rock slide. They were replaced with metal steps just east of the original site.

5. **The East Escarpment Stairs** at the foot of Kenilworth Access were completed in 2008. At the midway point, the 386 steps offer access to the Bruce and Rail Trails.

escarpment and valleys. Bayfront, Pier 4 Park, the Hamilton Harbour Waterfront Trail and Hamilton Beach Recreational Trail offer panoramic views of the Hamilton Harbour and northwest shoreline.

Enjoy the spectacular views of the lower city and harbour at Sam Lawrence Park, or relive history while visiting historic parks and museums such as Fieldcote, Dundurn, or Battlefield Park.

Source: City of Hamilton.

Devil's Punchbowl

The Devil's Punchbowl in Stoney Creek dates back at least 450 million years when it was created by fast-moving rivers that plunged over the escarpment. Reduction in the water flow left a beautiful 37 metre ribbon waterfall that falls into a large bowl-shaped 11 metre wide gorge, now famous with geologists worldwide for its exposed rock strata. The top of the bowl also provides visitors with a spectacular view of the harbour, the Skyway bridge and some incredible vegetation, and is located on the Bruce Trail.

Nobody is quite sure how the Devil's Punchbowl got its name, but legends are what make this landmark all the more intriguing. Some say that on dark, moonless nights, you can still see the glowing eyes of a ghostly moonshiner carrying two pails of booze along the top of the path leading to the bowl. Others believe there is a ghostly presence of a Boy Scout and his dog who got too close to the edge; the boy's father placed the first cross at the location. In reality, there have been numerous suicides at the Devil's Punchbowl.

Back in the 1930s, there was a large pine tree that was decorated annually for Christmas until it became too dangerously close to the edge of the bowl. Since then, a wooden cross and finally a large metal cross — made from a 50 m tall hydro tower — was erected to create feelings of goodwill among Hamiltonians. It was first lit only for Christmas and Easter, but thanks to the Knights of Columbus, is now lit every night of the year.

TREES

There are more than 120,000 trees located in Hamilton parks, open spaces and cemeteries. More than 300,000 street trees are also located within the road allowance of the 3,080 km of city roads. In addition to 560 park and shrub beds and another 420 beds on road allowances, the city values these assets at $375 million.

Battlefield Park

The Battle of Stoney Creek on June 6, 1813 was one of the most pivotal conflicts of the War of 1812. American forces would never again penetrate so far into the Niagara Peninsula.

The Battle at Stoney Creek pitted David against Goliath. More than 3,400 American troops invaded from the Niagara Peninsula and captured Fort George in Niagara-on-the-Lake before advancing to Stoney Creek. British troops, numbering only 700, retreated to Burlington Heights while the Americans took over the Gage Homestead for their headquarters.

A 19-year-old young woodsman, Billy Green — described as the Paul Revere of Canada by the *Hamilton Spectator* — managed to make his way through the American lines to warn the British of where exactly the Americans were located. The British used the information to launch a successful surprise attack.

The battle that only lasted for about 40 minutes resulted in hundreds of deaths and the capture of two American generals. In 1913, a monument was erected in the memory of those who died in the battle. Local school children were given a half-day off classes for the event and more than 15,000 people were in attendance.

Battlefield House, the former homestead of widow Mary Jones Gage and her two children, has been preserved as a museum and 34 acre Battlefield Park serves to preserve the memory of the battle.

Since 1981, history buffs have put on a re-enactment of the battle on the weekend nearest to the date of the actual battle. The half hour "battle" takes place on both Saturday and Sunday along with the Saturday Flag Day parade and a fireworks display after the Saturday evening enactment. Plans are already underway to celebrate the 200th anniversary of the battle in 2013.

COMMUNITY GARDENS

There are two community garden locations, one in West Hamilton and one in Dundas. The community gardens are available to all residents and do not use pesticides. Residents use the plots to grow their own vegetables and herbs. Rental fees are roughly $85 for a four-by-five-metre plot.

Take 5 CATHERINE GIBBON'S FIVE
FAVOURITE LANDSCAPES

Catherine Gibbon is a landscape painter who teaches at the Dundas Valley School of Art and who is represented by the Gallery on the Bay in Hamilton. These are five areas that provide her with inspiration for her landscapes:

1. The **Spencer Creek Wilderness Trail** off King St. W in Dundas just before the road goes up the escarpment. The trail goes up to the base of Webster's Falls and is about 12 m above the creek.

2. **The Sydenham Hill Lookout** on Sydenham Rd. in Dundas which affords a spectacular view of Dundas and all of Hamilton particularly at night.

3. **The Griffin Farm** at the corner of Mineral Spring Rd. and Sulphur Spring Rd. in Ancaster. This is an historic building and home of an ex-slave that is now a Black history museum.

4. **Crooks Hollow** in Greensville at Old Brock Rd. and Crooks Hollow Rd. in the area of the dam.

5. **The LaFarge Trail** at the 6th Concession and Middleton Rd. in Flamborough and on a drumlin which is a glacial deposit. It provides a panoramic view of the surrounding farms, streams and ponds.

ENVIRONMENTAL FOOTPRINT

Average number of hectares used to sustain a Canadian (also known as 'environmental footprint,' a measure of the resource use): 7.25

- Average number of hectares used by a Hamiltonian: 7.31
- Average number of hectares used by a Vancouverite: 7.31
- Average number of hectares used by a Torontonian: 7.36
- Average number of hectares used by a Calgarian: 9.86

Source: Federation of Canadian Municipalities.

The Royal Botanical Gardens

Partly in Hamilton and partly in neighbouring Burlington is Canada's largest botanical garden and one of the country's premier cultural, education and scientific institutions. The main presentation centre and some of its gardens are in Burlington but it originated in Hamilton in the late 1920s when the City of Hamilton began acquiring land for the beautification of the city's northwest entrance.

The Royal Botanical Gardens were established as an independent organization in 1941 with 486 hectares. In the late 1940s, the land base of the gardens had grown to almost 809 hectares. Today, it is comprised of five gardens; the Rock Garden with a display of annuals; the Arboretum with flowering shrubs and trees; the Laking Garden with perennials and ornamental grasses; Hendrie Park Gardens with shrubs and antique roses, annuals and perennials, and the RBG Centre with its orchid showcase and greenhouse displays of Mediterranean plants.

All the gardens' plants are all well documented and labelled for visitors. A spring highlight in Hamilton and surrounding areas (and for tourists from all over) is the annual lilac festival. The Arboretum has the world's largest collections of living lilacs and, when they all bloom, the view is breathtaking.

PLAY IT AGAIN!

- 17 indoor public swimming pools
- 10 outdoor public swimming pools
- 12 wading pools
- 43 splash pools
- 8 beaches
- 46 parks with baseball diamonds
- 27 parks with soccer pitches
- 16 parks with tennis courts
- 15 parks with bocce ball pits
- 3 public golf courses
- 137 km biking/hiking trails

Source: City of Hamilton.

Take 5 JIM HESLOP'S FIVE
GREAT BIRDWATCHING SITES

Jim Heslop is in charge of publicity for the Hamilton Naturalist Club and picked these spots with help from the book *Birds of Hamilton and Surrounding Territory* by Robert Currie. There are 387 different species of birds that have been identified in the area.

1. **Van Wagner's Beach** and the area around Hutch's Restaurant for migrating Arctic birds in the fall and for rare ocean birds from the East Coast.

2. **Dundas Valley** for Carolinian nesting birds.

3. **The Bruce Trail** along the top of the Escarpment from March to mid May when migrating hawks use the updraft from the Escarpment.

4. **Cootes Paradise Marsh** and the lands of the Royal Botanical Gardens for water birds and rare species.

5. **Fifty Point Conservation Area and the Waterfront Trail** along Lake Ontario.

SNOW

The city has available approximately 135 trucks, which can be dispatched for anti-icing, salting, sanding and/or plowing. The city also employs as many as 350 people during the snow season.

Take 5 FIVE HAMILTON WATERFALLS

Hamilton has over 60 waterfalls within city limits, and many of them are easily accessible even for those with disabilities. The following five are of particular interest and beauty.

1. **Webster's Falls** is one of the most stunning and easily accessed. The main falls has two overhanging drops. It is an easy five minute walk from the parking lot to view the falls from the top. More adventurous people can descend the stone stairs to the base and even hike down a path that takes people into the town of Dundas at the base of the Escarpment.

2. **Tew's Falls** is also nearby and can either be hiked or driven to. At 41 m, it is just a bit smaller than Niagara Falls. Much of the time, however, there is little water coming down. From the easily accessible viewing platform, you can see structure of the escarpment itself and a magnificent view down the gorge. A number of hiking trails are in the vicinity; the most popular of which is the one to Dundas Peaks, allowing you a picturesque view of the Dundas Valley below. This trail is very popular on Thanksgiving weekends when hundreds make the trek to see autumn colours.

DOWNTOWN

Hamilton's oldest area, its downtown core, has both charms and challenges. The challenges are pretty evident at even a quick glance. Boarded-up storefronts, weed-filled parking lots and dollar stores vie for space along many streets.

Massive urban renewal developments built over the last 40 years, such as Lloyd D. Jackson Square, Copps Coliseum and the Convention Centre fill the centre of the downtown core, although the indoor mall

3. **Sherman's Falls,** just off Lions Club Road in the old town of Ancaster, is estimated to be a mere three minute walk off the road but for most of the year it cannot be seen from the road because of the dense foliage. As a result, walking to it is of moderate difficulty but well worth it if it can be managed. This lovely waterfall has two cascading drops and is often referred to as Fairy Falls or Angel Falls. Sections of the Bruce Trail also cross this area.

4. **Felker's Falls** in the east end of the city is another moderately accessible waterfall 22 m high. It is not far from Battlefield Park and the adjacent escarpment area features trails, scenic vantage points, landscaping and the Peter Street Trail, a wheelchair accessible loop trail which travels through the conservation area

5. **Albion Falls** is the site of a grist mill that was built in 1792. Not far from the original location of the mill in King's Forest Park is one of the mill stones with a commemorative plaque. Rocks from the Albion Falls area were used in the construction of the Royal Botanical Gardens' Rock Garden. Legend has it that young Jane Riley, who was in love with Joseph Rousseau, stood at the top of a steep cliff not far from the falls and flung herself to the bottom, 30 metres below. The steep drop has since been dubbed "Lovers' Leap."

They Said It

"*My favourite thing about Hamilton is the harbour. It is peaceful, beautiful and unique. It also happens to epitomize the renaissance that faces the new Hamilton.*"

– Sheila Copps former MP from Hamilton East and deputy Prime Minister of Canada.

now boasts as much vacant space as the streetfront. Two significant historic structures — the Lister Block and the Royal Connaught Hotel — sit empty and deteriorating.

But while the signs of hope may not be as evident as the decay, they are still there. The city has recently inked a deal with LIUNA (the Labourers' International Union of North America) to restore the 120-year-old Lister Block, while Toronto developer Harry Stinson is flirting with the idea of a major restoration of the stately Connaught.

Hamilton's first skyscraper — the Piggot building — has been renovated into residential condominiums, while nearby, a new fountain graces Gore Park, the city's first public green space. The city is offering loans to bring more residential development downtown, while small sections of streets like James Street North and King William have undergone a revival in fortunes.

Did you know...

that because of the unique nature of the geology, Hamilton sits on the northern edge of the Carolinian Life Zone for trees? Hickory, sassafras and walnut trees give the area the look and feel of the southern U.S. These trees are in addition to the usual beech, maple and hemlock that are typical for the Great Lakes region.

They Said It

"Its grit outshines its glamour. My favourite thing about Hamilton (is) ... its size. Not too big, not too small. Big enough to get lost in and be anonymous, small enough so that you can make a splash and have people congratulate you on the street."

– John Terpstra, Hamilton author.

WHAT'S THERE:

- 10,160 residents
- 19,000 employees
- Hamilton City Hall
- Hamilton Art Gallery
- Copps Coliseum
- Hamilton Place
- The Farmer's Market
- McMaster University Continuing Education
- The Canadian Football Hall of Fame
- Sir John A. McDonald statue
- Cenotaph
- Statue of Queen Victoria
- 82 bars and restaurants
- 2 business improvement associations (BIAs)

Did you know...

that the City of Hamilton has a 28,500 sq. ft. greenhouse operation that produces over 500,000 seedlings annually? In addition, it maintains 70,000 sq. ft of traffic island planting beds (245 locations) and 58,500 sq. ft. of floral displays (196 planting beds), 477 planters and 440 hanging baskets.

> *"People don't necessarily feel safe because there's not people walking around...James Street has had a sordid history, but I think it's an interesting history, it's part of what makes the street special."*
> **– Don Kuruc, James St. N shop owner,**
> **in reference to the downtown core.**

WASTING AWAY

Hamiltonians put out 13,500 tons less waste at curbside in 2007 compared to the previous year. City garbage crews collected 216,000 tons of garbage, blue box recyclables, organics and yard waste in 2007 and that was down from 229,500 tons in 2006. Only 126,000 tons went into landfills which represented a reduction of 2 percent. The percentage of garbage that was diverted from landfills went up from 40.1 percent to 41.7 percent. The long range goal is to divert 65 percent of garbage from landfills.

WASTE MANAGEMENT INVENTORY

- 1 landfill-active
- 12 closed landfills
- 3 transfer stations
- 3 community recycling centres
- 1 leaf & yard waste site
- 1 central composting
- 1 future alternative disposal facility

Source: City of Hamilton.

TRANSIT SYSTEMS BY THE NUMBERS

- Number of routes: 30
- Number of bus stops: 2,200
- Number of buses: 204
- Number of bus shelters: 513
- Annual number of boarding passengers: 21,000,000

- Revenue earned in 2006: $34 million from fare box, advertising and subsidies
- Fare: $2.40 cash; $1.85 adult ticket; $1.50 student ticket
- Total area covered: $1,117.2$ km^2

FOR SHORE

In 1990, less than five percent Hamilton's shorelines were accessible to the public. Much of the south shore was industrial and fenced. By 2005, 25 percent of the shoreline was accessible to the public. New access was created and enhanced at LaSalle Park, Northeast Shoreline, Bayfront Park, Pier 4 Park, Hamiltonian Pier, and the Harbour Waterfront Trail connecting Cootes Paradise through to Pier 8.

Source: Hamilton Harbour Remedial Action Plan.

Weblinks

The Niagara Escarpment

http://www.escarpment.org/
Administrative and historical information on the escarpment.

The Hamilton Conservation Authority

http://www.conservationhamilton.ca/
The region's largest environmental management agency website will tell you all about the trails and waterfalls in the area.

The Royal Botanical Gardens

http://www.rbg.ca/pages/visit_explore.html
History and description of the more than 2,700 gardens with schedule of events, hours of operation, and practically everything else you'd want to know before visiting.

Weather and Climate

Located at the western end of Lake Ontario, Hamilton has a mild climate compared to many Canadian cities. Warm summers and cold winters are influenced by Lake Ontario, as well as by the Niagara Escarpment, known locally as the Mountain. Virtually splitting the city in two, the escarpment reduces the effect of warm southerly winds, making the lower section of Hamilton cooler in the summer months and milder in the winter. However there is one drawback to this — the escarpment also contributes to more smog downtown than in the southern section of Hamilton during the summer months.

In addition, Lake Ontario and Lake Erie (approximately 60 miles to the south) are a factor in creating extremely humid conditions during the summer. During the warmer months, Hamilton's temperature often reaches into the 30s. Winters are relatively cool, but not unbearable, with January daytime temperatures frequently rising above zero. Average snowfall is about 113 cm, but varies considerably from year to year.

AVERAGE DAILY TEMPERATURES (°C)
MAX

Jan	Feb	Mar	Apr	May	Jun	Jul	Aug	Sep	Oct	Nov	Dec
-2.2	-1.2	4.0	11.2	18.5	23.7	26.3	25.1	20.7	13.8	7.0	0.9

MIN

Jan	Feb	Mar	Apr	May	Jun	Jul	Aug	Sep	Oct	Nov	Dec
-9.7	-9.1	-4.5	1.2	7.3	12.4	15.1	14.5	10.2	4.4	-0.4	-6.2

Source: Environment Canada.

Take 5 — MATT HAYES TALKS ABOUT THE WEATHER

Matt Hayes, the personable weatherman on CHCH-TV, is a Hamilton icon, known for his great sense of humour and community involvement. He refers to himself as "the complaints department for Mother Nature" and shares these observations about his experiences.

1. It's funny that the sports guy is never blamed when the Ti-Cats lose. The anchorman never has to answer for the war in Iraq. But the weather guy always has to take it on the chin for a lousy weekend. It's either too wet or too dry, or too hot or too cold.

2. A woman once called to tell me I ruined a picnic for a group of underprivileged children with "my rain."

3. A guy called me once to ask what he should wear. I told him to wear the blue suit because I always liked him in it.

4. As weatherman, I'm a one-issue guy. I always have to be prepared with a forecast. People aren't interested in my views on anything else.

5. I'm also supposed to be a psychic. Every six months or so I get asked as question like, "What's it going to be like on September 30th? I'm getting married that day and I want it to be nice."

AND THE WINNER IS . . .

- Record high: 41.1°C on July 14, 1868
- Record low: -30.6°C on January 25, 1884
- Record rainfall in one day: 107 mm on July 26, 1989
- Record snowfall in one day: 43.2 cm on January 22, 1966
- Record wind speed: reached 93 km/hour November 11, 1988
- Record wind gust: 133 km on January 26, 1978
- Record wind chill: -43°C on, January 19, 1994
- Record humidex: 49.1°C on July 14, 1991

Take 5 FIVE WEATHER-DEPENDENT ACTIVITIES

1. **Hamilton Winterfest's** city-wide events include a number of outdoor events including ice bowling and snowshoeing at the Hamilton Children's Museum in January.

2. **The Royal Botanical Garden's Lilac Festival** in May features the world's largest collection of lilacs.

3. **Nothing beats ice cream in hot summer weather.** Westfield Village's annual Ice Cream Festival has something for young and old, including historic handmade ice cream.

4. **Winona Peach Festival** has celebrated the juicy, golden goodness of local peaches for more than 40 years.

5. **Ice climbing!** Frigid weather, waterfalls and the escarpment combine to make a challenging sport overseen locally by the Hamilton Conservation Authority and the Alpine Club of Canada.

Take 5 FIVE HAMILTON STREET NAMES
EVOKING SEASONS OR CLIMATE

1. **Autumn Leaf Road**, Dundas
2. **Spring Street**, Hamilton
3. **Summer Place**, Hamilton
4. **Sun Avenue**, Flamborough
5. **Windrush Crescent**, Hamilton

FEELING HOT, HOT, HOT

Hamilton's average summer temperature is 25.03°C, placing it 21st in a list of 100 Canadian cities. Leading the pack is Kamloops, with an average temperature of 26.94°C. Toronto, ranked ninth, has an average of 25.38°C, while Prince Rupert at the bottom of the list is a comparatively cool 15.67°C.

HERE COMES THE SUN

Hamilton is among the sunniest spots in the country all year round, with an average of 302 sunny days per year. This makes it 34th out of 100 Canadian cities, but less than 10 percent behind the leader, Kamloops, which has 333 sunny days annually.

It ranks 23rd out of 100 for sunny summer days, with 831 hours of sunshine. Yellowknife receives 1,034 hours of sunshine, making it Canada's sunniest summer city, but you're not likely to get much of a suntan in Prince Rupert, which has only 445 sunny summer hours.

Did you know...

that many migratory birds rely on thermals — columns of rising hot air — to allow them to glide great distances with little effort? In the spring, thermals are a rarity over the cold waters of the Great Lakes. To navigate around the lakes, migrating birds, including hawks and other raptors, often follow the escarpment.

Hurricane Hazel hits Hamilton

On October 5, 1954, Hurricane Hazel was spotted off the coast of Grenada. As the storm made its way north and west, Canadians braced themselves.

The Hamilton weather office issued a warning at noon on October 15. According to a *Spectator* report, the weather office cautioned, "the effects of Hurricane Hazel will be felt in this city and district late this afternoon and tonight. Wind velocity will gradually increase during the afternoon and evening." Meteorologists predicted the wind would average 72 km per hour, with gusts up to 120 km per hour.

By late afternoon, Hamilton was being blasted by sheets of rain and heavy winds. Traffic slowed to a crawl. As emergency crews mobilized, the storm worsened. By 10 pm it was dangerous to go outside — tree branches, fences, just about anything that was not solidly anchored was likely to fly through the air, propelled by the winds.

On the escarpment, a small avalanche of loose soil and rock tumbled onto the Sherman Cut. Meanwhile, boats were being tossed about in the harbour. At least three boats sunk, while others were tossed ashore or smashed against piers.

In the city's east end, residents battled the fury of Lake Ontario. Men worked all through the night, piling sandbags in a makeshift dykes, while women kept them supplied with coffee and sandwiches. Despite their efforts, waves rolled across the road, surrounding many of the houses on the lakeside.

Flooding created serious problems elsewhere in the city, as the ground was already saturated from previous rains. At the TH&B railway underpasses on James and John Street, the water was so high that the streets were barely passable. On many roads, water was up to the hubcaps of cars. On the Mountain, standing water created small lakes, including one on East 38th Street that was rumored to be 4.5 m deep.

Across Ontario, 1,800 families lost their homes as a result of Hazel. Eighty-one people, many of them from Toronto, were killed. Property damage was estimated at $25 million — roughly the equivalent of $170 million in 2008.

Compared to some other places, Hamilton was relatively unscathed. Property damage was estimated at $1 million and there were no fatalities. "It could have been worse," the *Spectator* reported on October 15, "and was worse elsewhere."

They Said It

"I went into Town in the sleigh for papa. We have had an immense fall of snow. We were almost snowed up. It is the greatest fall of snow that has been known for many years."

– 13-year-old Sophia MacNab, daughter of Sir Allan Napier MacNab February 16, 1846.

HUMIDITY

With Lake Ontario right on its doorstep, Hamilton is definitely prone to humidity. In fact, it's the fourth most humid city in Canada, trailing just slightly behind Windsor, Sarnia and Kingston. On 54 days of the year, the humidex rating in Hamilton hits 30 or more, and on 16 of those days it is above 35.

SMOKE AND HAZE (AND FOG)

Although Hamilton has sunny days about 83 percent of the time, it also has one of the highest rates of smoke and haze. The city ranks fourth, with 100 days a year of smoke or haze. Windsor, London and Brantford, respectively, take the top places for this category. Hamilton also gets a lot of fog — 44 days per year — which places it 17th. Not surprisingly, St. John's, NL is the fog capital of Canada with 119 foggy days per year. But compare that to Penticton, BC residents, who experience it just two days annually.

Did you know...

that a severe winter storm struck in December 1944, making roads in the Hamilton area nearly impassable? One woman in labour spent four hours in a horse-drawn sleigh between Stoney Creek and Vinemount in order to meet with the ambulance that would take her to a maternity hospital. And a soldier stricken with an acute attack of appendicitis while travelling by bus to Niagara Falls was taken part of the way to hospital by a toboggan pulled by a horse.

Take 5 — KATHY RENWALD'S FIVE
GREAT GARDEN WALKS

Award winning journalist and television personality Kathy Renwald is a Master Gardener, gardening columnist and author of the best-selling books, *Annuals and Perennials for Ontario* and *Tree and Shrub Gardening for Ontario*. Kathy notes Hamilton, especially the areas below the escarpment, is blessed with a climate mild enough to experiment in growing a wide range of plants, including flowering dogwoods, Carolina silverbells, and Magnolia tripetala (umbrella magnolia).

1. **The Royal Botanical Gardens** on our doorstep. Visit the Rock Garden in spring or fall and be treated to layers of colour. Tulips and daffodils in spring; gigantic willows, Japanese maples and evergreens forming a fall canopy. There's a world famous lilac collection at the Arboretum, and iris and peonies at the Laking Garden.

2. **Front yard gardens**. Walk the Durand neighborhood or the North End and see front yard gardens with the individual stamp of Hamiltonians. Whimsical, passionate, enthused and informed gardens make walking a treat and an adventure.

3. **The Waterfront Trail on Lake Ontario**. Vintage cottages and summer homes from the turn of the century display their one-of-a-kind gardens to trail walkers. The lake on one side, gardens on the other, how can you miss?

4. **The Kitchen Garden at Dundurn Castle** and the period garden at Whitehern. They are historical gems in the middle of the city; Whitehern is a refuge from hectic urban life, Dundurn is a treasure chest of heirloom edibles.

5. **Our local nurseries.** You can buy some of the best trees, shrubs and perennials here, as well as "untreated seeds", vintage roses and unusual annuals at our specialist nurseries.

They Said It

> "The giant rollers ended up right across the road ... For years after, I had occasional bad dreams of the lake flooding on and on and endangering everything below the escarpment."
>
> **– Muriel Gray Utter, eyewitness to Hurricane Hazel at Van Wagner's Beach.**

GROWING SEASON

The Hamilton area is a great place for gardeners and farmers. Most years the area has about 138 frost-free days, starting around April 29 and ending around October 15. In addition, good soil, the availability of good water, and the moderating effects of Lake Ontario and the escarpment help make it an excellent area for growing a range of produce, including tender fruits and vegetables.

PRECIPITATION

- Total annual precipitation: 910.1 mm
- Annual rainfall: 764.8 mm
- Annual snowfall: 161.8 cm
- Percentage of precipitation that falls as snow: 17.8
- August is the wettest month of the year, but December is the second with a combined total of 83 mm of snow and rain. November is third with a combined total of 80 mm.

Source: Environment Canada.

Did you know...

that with its mild climate, Hamilton is close to the northernmost border of the Carolinian forest zone? This allows a number of trees normally found in more southern regions to flourish here, including sassafras, shagbark hickory, tulip tree, honey locust and Kentucky coffee tree.

Blackout

Hot August weather was one of the factors in a blackout affecting 50 million people across Ontario and the eastern United States in 2003. Operational problems at an Ohio power company added to the problem as well. According to an Environment Canada report, the summer heat, combined with low winds that prevented cooling, expanded power lines. The lines sagged, caught in tree branches and ultimately interrupted electrical transmission.

It was the most widespread blackout since 1965. At 4:11 on the afternoon of Thursday, August 14, 100 power plants and 15 transmission lines serving Ontario and several American states stopped working.

In Hamilton, the afternoon commute was just getting underway. People who found themselves low on gas discovered there was no way to refuel without electricity, and no way to get money out of cash machines either.

Drivers had to contend with the lack of streetlights. Most were courteous and cooperative, patiently waiting their turn to advance at intersections. In some locations, civilians stepped in to direct traffic. Appreciative drivers offered them cold drinks, food, or orange safety vests.

Meanwhile, city authorities doubled the number of policemen on duty and also called in volunteer fire fighters. There were some fears of looting, but the crime rate actually dropped during the blackout.

Anxious city residents stocked up on essentials, including drinking water and ice for refrigerators and freezers. But restaurants and grocery stores threw out tens of thousands of dollars of perishable food. There were also worries about dwindling water supplies, so emergency water measures were put into effect.

At the Hamilton Airport, flights were grounded, stranding about 700 travelers overnight.

It was 21 hours before power was restored, and even then Hamiltonians were cautioned that rolling blackouts would likely occur for the next few days.

When it was all over, Hamilton estimated the cost at more than $2 million, a large portion of it overtime pay for emergency staff.

IT'S RAINING, IT'S POURING

With an average annual rainfall of 765 mm, Hamilton is the 44th rainiest city in Canada. Nearby Guelph and Kitchener-Waterloo placed 42nd and 43rd, respectively, while Toronto ranked 58th. Prince Rupert is the rainiest city in Canada, while Whitehorse is the least rainy. In Hamilton there's likely to be some rain on 195 days of the year, but on 118 of those days the rain will be less than 5 mm. The heaviest rainfalls tend to be in August, when an average of 86.5 mm falls, followed by July and June.

Take 5 FIVE SEVERE STORMS

1. **1845:** Among the earliest recorded snowstorms in Hamilton was a blizzard in February 1845. Three days of continuous snow made the roads nearly impassable. The stagecoach from Toronto to Hamilton took two days to complete its journey.

2. **1878:** Starting September 8, rain poured down on Hamilton for a steady 70 hours, flooding roads and creating havoc.

3. **1898:** Snow began to fall on December 4, continued all day and into the night. Then the mercury dropped and winds picked up, breaking branches, telephone and hydro poles. Hamilton was completely cut off from the outside world and without electricity for close to 36 hours.

4. **1955:** On the weekend of August 13-14, Hurricane Connie hit Hamilton, smashing boats and cottages and leaving at least 18 homeless.

5. **1973:** Between April 9 and 10, gale-force winds and flooding drove people out of their homes in Hamilton's east-end beach strip and Saltfleet Township. Saltfleet was declared a disaster area.

CH-CH-CHILLY

In a ranking of 100 coldest Canadian cities, Hamilton was 82nd, just slightly cooler than Kelowna, which placed 80th. The coldest city in Canada, year-round is Yellowknife. Hamilton's coldest month of the year is January, with an average daily temperature of -6°C. The temperature drops below -20°C about four days per year, but is lower than 0°C on an average of 142 days per year. Still, Hamilton's winters are milder than that of most Canadian cities, with a ranking of 27 out of 100. The mildest winter weather in the country can be found in Victoria, the harshest in Yellowknife.

PASS THE SHOVEL

January is the snowiest month with 43.2 cm of the white stuff, followed by December with 36.8 cm and February with 35.2 cm. Snow cover is deepest in January and February, at an average of 9 cm. Compared to 99 other Canadian cities, Hamilton has it pretty good, ranking 54 out 100 for overall snowfall.

Gander, NL is the country's snowiest city, followed by Corner Brook and Sept-Iles, QC. At the bottom of the list is Victoria. Hamilton's greatest snowfall on record was January 26, 1966, when 43.2 cm of snow fell in a single day. The greatest depth of snow recorded was on February 7, 1978, with 64 cm of snow on the ground. Hamilton has snow cover of 1 cm or more for an average of 82 days each year.

As for actual snow days, Hamilton is in the middle of the pack,

Did you know...

that a sudden squall was responsible for one of Hamilton's most important heritage treasures? On the night of August 7, 1813, two American ships, the *Hamilton* and the *Scourge,* were sunk in Lake Ontario during an unexpected storm, with the loss of many men. Now in 100 meters of water the two boats are considered the only entire War of 1812 vessels in existence and are being protected for posterity.

Quake, Rattle and Roll

A number of earthquakes have been felt in Hamilton. Records date back to 1867, when a quake estimated at 6.5 on the Richter scale occurred at the mouth of the Saguenay River, Quebec. Tremors were felt hundreds of miles away in Hamilton.

Other earthquakes have come a little closer to home. Nearby Burlington was the epicentre of a mild one, with a magnitude of 2.0 on December 3, 1979. Seven weeks later, on January 21, 1980, a second earthquake of the same magnitude started in East Hamilton.

Compared to the Pacific coast, Hamilton is relatively earthquake free, but the area does have two fault lines, one of them in the Dundas Valley. According to one seismologist with Natural Resources Canada, there are usually two or three quakes a year at the western end of Lake Ontario. Every now and then, seismic activity is strong enough for tremors to be felt and a little damage done.

On September 4, 1944, masonry from the spire of St. Paul's Presbyterian Church, James Street, was shaken loose during an earthquake.

On September 25, 1998, another church spire was damaged in an earthquake. Stones in the tower of All Saints Anglican Church on Queen Street North were shaken loose in an earthquake that registered 5.4 on the Richter scale. Tremors were felt as far away as Trenton, Ontario. The quake's epicentre was 170 kilometers southwest of Hamilton, south of Lake Erie and close to the border between Ohio and Pennsylvania.

That was the most severe earthquake in Hamilton in recent years. At Hamilton Place, mirrors rattled. Dishes shook in cupboards and cabinets. An 11-year-old boy in Stoney Creek fell out of bed when the quake hit.

Tremors started at 3:52 pm, prompting a flurry of calls to 911. No property damage or personal injuries were reported, but many people were frightened. Others were simply curious about what was happening.

Early in 2008 another quake hit Hamilton. This one was much closer — 5 km southeast of downtown. It hit at 6:56 am and was accompanied by a loud popping noise. This bang (or boom) was the result of some of the quake's energy being released into the atmosphere and can often be heard close to the epicentre. Fortunately, the January 2008 earthquake registered at a comparatively mild 2.0. Anything over 5 is considered strong enough to cause structural damage.

ranked 50th, with 56 snow days a year. Val d'Or, QC gets snow on 104 days throughout the year, with Gander, NL following closely at 102 days. Meanwhile, Victoria and Duncan, BC get away with just snowfall on just 10 days of the year.

WHITE CHRISTMAS

If you're in Iqaluit, Whitehorse, Timmins or Quebec City you're pretty much guaranteed a white Christmas, with at least 2 cm of snow on the ground. If you really need a white Christmas fix, Sault Ste. Marie is your best bet, where there's a 70 percent chance of snow falling on Christmas day and a 93 percent chance of at least 2 cm of snow on the ground. In Hamilton, the odds drop to 68 percent. Chances of a picture-perfect Christmas, with snow on the ground and more falling are even lower, at just 26 percent.

PAYING FOR WINTER

- 2007 budget for "winter control": $20,400,000
- Approximate number of employees: 350
- Number of vehicles in Hamilton's winter control fleet: 135

Source: City of Hamilton.

WIND

Hamilton is the windiest city in Ontario and ranks at 11th place nationwide. The windiest Canadian cities are St. John's and Gander. Ontario cities that make the list include St. Catharines-Niagara in 14th place, Kingston at 17, and Windsor at 18. In Hamilton there are 34 days of the year when the wind blows at 52

Did you know...

that a tornado touched down in Hamilton on November 9, 2005, toppling trees and ripping the roof off an elementary school? Environment Canada officials said it was very rare for a tornado to occur so late in the year.

km/hour or more. January has the strongest winds of any month, blowing at an average speed of 21.2 km/hour.

LIGHTNING

Shocking! When it comes to lightning, Hamilton is one of the most active Canadian cities, with 191 lightning flashes per year per 100 square km. Windsor leads with 251, followed by Toronto at 200. Inuvik, NT, is at the bottom of the list with just one lighting flash annually per 100 square km. However, when it comes to the actual number of days when there are thunderstorms, Hamilton is 14th on the list of 100, with Windsor and Toronto leading.

WINTERFEST

Marking its 30th anniversary in 2008, Hamilton Winterfest is an annual two-week celebration of winter and winter fun. Across the city, a varied combination of events offer something for just about everyone and the image of Chimo, the snowman that is the Winterfest mascot, seems to be just about everywhere.

Free live concerts, lumberjack competitions, skating, snowshoeing, art exhibits, contests and demonstrations are just some of the activities. In many cases, activities are free, thanks to generous sponsorship from community businesses and other organizations.

VALENTINE'S DAY

Valentine's Day is traditionally one of the busiest days for florists, but in 2007 Mother Nature put a major crimp in their plans. A huge winter storm wreaked havoc from Louisiana to Quebec, with tornadoes,

Did you know...

that when Hurricane Connie hit Hamilton in August 1955, a tugboat called Youville broke loose at the foot of Ferguson Street? Wind and waves bounced her around against nearby vessels. To prevent further damage, the navy sank her.

heavy snowfalls, ice pellets and severe wind chills. Winter weather hit hardest in Hamilton, Ontario, where 30.4 cm of snow fell on February 13th — breaking all previous records for daily snowfall in February. On February 14, the snow continued, dumping another 16 cm and breaking another record for snow on Valentine's Day. Together, the storm accounted for the greatest two-day snowfall ever in Hamilton.

Florists had already drafted extra drivers to handle the holiday delivery. As they braced for the storm, they increased the number of drivers in hopes of completing their deliveries. But the storm created chaos on the roads, with at least 1,000 accidents across southern Ontario and a 70-car pile-up near neighbouring Ancaster.

Weblinks

Weather Winners Website
http://www.on.ec.gc.ca/weather/winners/intro-e.html
David Phillips, Senior Climatologist and Environment Canada analyzed weather trends for the past 30 years and ranked 100 Canadian cities. Find out where your city fits in any one of 72 categories, including hottest, coldest, driest, wettest and windiest.

Canada's Top Ten Weather Stories
http://www.msc.ec.gc.ca/media/top10/index_e.html
Another Environment Canada site with listings compiled by David Phillips. Fascinating stories about the past year's top weather events — and the runners-up. Brief regional stories provide plenty of details about more localized weather.

National Climate Data and Information Archive
http://climate.weatheroffice.ec.gc.ca/Welcome_e.html
Find out what the weather was like on a particular day, or compare historic weather conditions, including precipitation, humidity, heat and cold in cities across the country.

WARNING

LOUD NOISE
HORNS CAN
SOUND AT
ANY TIME

Economy

Strategically situated on the western tip of Lake Ontario about 80 kilometres from both Toronto and the U.S. border, Hamilton is the geographical center of the largest commercial and industrial area of the country, an area that has come to be known as the "Golden Horseshoe." Within a day's truck drive of the city are an estimated 120 million people. Goods can be shipped and raw materials received from a mature network of expressways, rail lines, shipping on the St. Lawrence Seaway and air.

Steel, of course, dominates the city's economic landscape. Close to 60,000 people work directly or indirectly in the steel industry, so as steel goes so goes Hamilton. Although steel and its counterpart manufacturing continue to be the city's largest sectors, the number of people working in them has declined in recent decades.

Like many industrial cities, Hamilton is dealing with the rise of the service sector. Thanks in large part to McMaster University, the health services sector in the city has grown exponentially. Indeed the Hamilton Health Sciences Corporation employs nearly 10,000 people. The McMaster Biosciences Incubation Centre located in the Michael G. DeGroote centre is filled to capacity with researchers and start-up life sciences companies. The research transition facility offers more than 7,000 sq. ft. of wet and dry lab space designed to support and accelerate commercialization efforts.

McMaster University is also an important economic engine for the community. In addition to 3,500 full-time staff and 27,000 students, the university is overseeing McMaster Innovation Park. Construction of the CANMET-MTL (the federal government's materials technology laboratory) will begin in the park this year and is expected to open in 2010. Mohawk College of Applied Arts and Technology also provides a crucial link to industry and a technical resource not available in many communities of comparable size.

High technology companies and biotechnology clusters have also begun to emerge as legitimate industries rather than public relations talk. Agriculture continues to be a mainstay. Key economic issues facing the city include a potential U.S. recession, but also putting in place the infrastructure to ensure that Hamilton is nimble enough to take advantage of a business looking to relocate from Toronto and nearby American cities as well as continuing to focus on economic diversity.

GDP

Gross Domestic Product (GDP) represents the total value of goods and services produced.

- Ontario's 2006 GDP: $490 billion
- Hamilton accounts for six percent of the province GDP or $29.4 billion
- Percentage accounted for by the service sector: 67.6
- Percentage accounted for the good producing sector: 32.4

Source: Statistics Canada.

Did you know...

That during the early part of the 19th century Hamilton was overshadowed by nearby Dundas? The opening of the Burlington Canal in 1830 changed all that. It provided the link from Hamilton Harbour to Lake Ontario, leading to its establishment as an important port and rail centre.

Steel City

Hamilton's early economic history was in large measure determined by its geographic good luck. For early settlers, it had some of the richest farmland in the country. For the industry that would come later, it had access to natural resources (dolomite, limestone, and of course, its natural harbour on Lake Ontario) along with its location in the middle of what would later be dubbed the Golden Horseshoe.

It also had a strong measure of political good fortune. Strong tariffs imposed by Sir John A. Macdonald's government motivated a group of opportunistic New York City venture capitalists to come northward to Hamilton. They saw huge profit potential in steel and from 1893 onward the steel industry and Hamilton's economy were forever intertwined.

Two steel companies have had a towering influence on the city. In 1910, with the Canadian steel industry considering its future, five companies came together to form what would be the Steel Company of Canada or Stelco. The other major player, is Dofasco. Dofasco had its beginnings in 1912, when C.W. Sherman founded the Dominion Steel Casting Company to manufacture castings for Canadian railways. Later named Dominion Foundries and Steel, the company's name was officially changed to Dofasco in 1980.

Hamilton still accounts for 40 percent of Canada's steelmaking capacity. (Another 15 percent is located within a 50-kilometre radius of the city.) The industry employs some 16,000 people in city directly either in steelmaking or processing. More than 500 firms are also directly or indirectly involved in the industry and another 57,000 people are employed in the general manufacturing sector.

The steel landscape in Hamilton has changed dramatically in the last two years. After two years of court-ordered bankruptcy protection, Stelco's Hilton & Lake Erie works were bought by the giant U.S. Steel. The biggest shock occurred, however, when Dofasco was bought by Arcelor Steel, which in turn was purchased by Mittal, the world's largest steel company. A number of smaller mergers and acquisitions have also had an impact in the city.

Throughout all of the global turmoil, what is remarkable is that Hamilton has remained a steel city. The next chapter in the history of the city, and that of the steel which has helped to build it, is yet to be written. What that chapter is likely to contain, very few are willing to guess.

Take 5 FIVE HAMILTON SALARIES
(2007)

1. **Murray Martin**, CEO of Hamilton Health Science: $676,022
2. **Kevin Smith**, CEO of St Joseph's Health Centre: $640,000
3. **Peter George**, President of McMaster University: $504,792
4. **Marilynn West-Moynes**, President of Mohawk College: $278,702
5. **Christopher Spence**, Director of Education on the Hamilton School Board: $210,012

Source: Hamilton Spectator.

TAXES

- Provincial sales tax: 8 percent
- GST (federal sales tax): 5 percent
- Personal income tax rates: 14 percent of taxable income
- Small business tax rate: 11 percent
- Corporate tax rate: 19.5 percent

Source: Canada Customs and Revenue Agency.

INFLATION

At the end of April 2008, the Canadian inflation rate had increased 1.6 percent from a year earlier. In the same period, Ontario's increase was 1.3 percent higher.

They Said It

"The people in Hamilton have great attitudes and we have found that they like living in Hamilton and are happy to work here."
> **– Dan Plashkes, CEO of SP Data on moving his company operation to Hamilton.**

You Said How Much?

All figures are hourly and are drawn from the latest available data.

General practitioners	$54.03
Optometrists	$45.28
University professors	$34.20
Occupational therapists	$32.70
Registered nurses	$32.46
Police officers	$32.35
Lawyers	$31.80
Physiotherapists	$30.66
Pharmacists	$29.28
Computer engineers	$28.01
Electrical engineers	$28.00
Bricklayers	$27.70
Civil engineers	$27.60
Senior managers, health care	$27.39
Social workers	$27.00
Secondary school teachers	$26.83
Electricians	$26.30
Financial auditors and accountants	$26.22
Financial managers	$25.81
Plumbers	$23.30
Banking managers	$22.50
Crane operators	$22.00
Letter carriers	$21.47
Executive assistants	$21.10
Heavy equipment mechanics	$20.38
Insurance agents	$19.30
Graphic designers	$17.70
Medical secretaries	$16.80
Legal secretaries	$16.50
Auto mechanics	$16.50
Retail trade managers	$15.23
Restaurant managers	$14.56
Artisans and craft persons	$11.25
Cooks	$11.10

Source: Human Resources and Development Canada.

TAX FREEDOM DAY

National Tax Freedom Day (the date on which earnings no longer go to taxes, 2008) is June 14.

- Alberta: May 28
- New Brunswick: June 3
- Prince Edward Island: June 4
- Manitoba: June 8

Tim Horton's

In 1964, Toronto Maple Leafs star defenseman Tim Horton opened a doughnut shop with partner Jim Charade. They already owned several chicken and burger joints in Toronto, but the businesses were struggling because of competition from larger chains.

At the time, a place which sold only coffee, tea and doughnuts was a novelty. Horton and Charade chose Hamilton for their first shop primarily because land was cheaper than in Toronto and parking was more readily available. Their first location in a converted service station at 65 Ottawa Street gave them an extra edge, because it was close to Hamilton's steel industry. Twice a day, right around the time steelworkers changed shifts, Tim Horton's produced a batch of fresh, baked-in-store doughnuts. The new coffee shop quickly became popular — and very, very profitable.

Tim Horton was busy being a professional hockey player and Jim Charade got involved in other businesses, so in 1965, Charade sold out his shares to Ron Joyce, a Hamilton policeman and Dairy Queen franchise owner who loved Horton's doughnuts. Joyce became the first franchisee in a chain that would grow to more than 2,000 stores across Canada and the U.S.

Joyce has not forgotten his Hamilton roots. In 1998, he donated $5 million to Hamilton Place, which resulted in it being renamed Ronald V. Joyce Centre for the Performing Arts at Hamilton. In 2005 he donated another $10 million towards a new sports stadium at McMaster University, and has also donated $2 million for scholarships and $10 million towards a proposed Burlington Campus. His efforts have earned him numerous honours, including humanitarian awards and membership in the Order of Canada.

- **Ontario: June 9**
- Nova Scotia: June 12
- British Columbia: June 13
- Quebec: June 19
- Saskatchewan: June 20
- Newfoundland and Labrador: June 30

Source: Fraser Institute.

HOUSEHOLD INCOME

The median household income in Canada after taxes was $45,900 in 2005. Here's how it breaks down across some selected cities:

- Calgary $56,600
- Toronto $55,400
- Hamilton $52,300
- Vancouver $49,200
- Winnipeg $44,900
- Halifax $42,900
- Quebec City $42,000
- Montreal $40,700

Source: Canada Mortgage and Housing Corporation.

Take 5 FIVE TIM HORTON FACTS

1. Tim Horton developed his love for doughnuts while playing with the Pittsburgh Hornets.
2. Apple fritters, Dutchies and Chocolate Walnut-Crunch doughnuts were among the innovations introduced at Tim Horton's.
3. Timbits were introduced in 1976.
4. The first "Roll Up the Rim to Win" contest was launched in February 1986. The slogan was coined by Ron Buist, the company's marketing director.
5. Tim Horton's children's camps are located in Parry Sound, Ontario (1975), Tatamagouche, Nova Scotia (1988); Kananaskis, Alberta (1991); Quyon, Quebec (1994) Campbellsville, Kentucky (2001) and St. George, Ontario (2002).

WHERE THE MONEY GOES IN ONTARIO

Ontario households spent an average of $73,318 a year in 2006. Here's how it broke down:

- Income tax: $14,869 (20.3 percent)
- Shelter: $15,163 (20.7 percent)
- Transportation: $9,645 (13.2 percent)
- Food: $7,331 (10.0 percent)
- Insurance/pension payments: $3,977(5.4 percent)
- Household operation: $3,429 (4.7 percent)
- Clothing: $3,185 (4.3 percent)
- Monetary gifts/contributions: $1,808 (2.5 percent)

Take 5 JOHN DOLBEC'S FIVE GOOD
REASONS FOR DOING BUSINESS IN HAMILTON

John Dolbec has been the executive director of the Hamilton and District Chamber of Commerce since 1988. Before that he had spent more than 25 years in the private sector, mostly as a banker with the Bank of Montreal.

1. Hamilton is a relatively low costs business service provider with low development charges, land prices, relatively low cost supply chain, and otherwise competitive taxes.
2. Ninety percent of all business decisions impacting Hamilton are made right in Hamilton by Hamiltonians.
3. Highly trained, well-educated and well-motivated work force.
4. Very high quality of life.
5. Geography with one of the finest natural harbours in North America linked to ground, road, rail and air transportation assets that can effectively reach a market of 120 million people within one day's truck travel of Hamilton.

- Health care: $1,609 (2.2 percent)
- Tobacco and alcohol: $537 (0.7 percent)
- Education: $1,402 (1.9 percent)
- Personal care: $1,233 (1.7 percent)
- Reading material: $268 (0.4 percent)
- Games of chance: $262 (0.4 percent)

Source: Statistics Canada.

Take 5 FIVE GROUNDBREAKING
HAMILTON STRIKES

1. **1833:** A group of disgruntled printers go on strike in the first union action in Hamilton, and one of the earliest in Canada.

2. **1856:** Over 500 employees working in the Great West Railways yards walk out over the dismissal of a worker who was replaced with the friend of a foreman. Although the worker was rehired to settle the dispute, the employees didn't succeed in their quest to have the foreman fired.

3. **1866:** Hamilton foundry owners battle the Molders Union and attempt to blacklist union men. A resulting 11-month long strike sees the union disappear after losing the support of workers. It is active again, however, by 1874.

4. **1906:** The 180 drivers for the Hamilton Street Railway (HSR) strike for improved wages and the recognition of their union. A violent strike, which sees streetcars driven by replacement drivers attacked by rock-throwing mobs estimated in newspaper reports at 15,000, the dispute causes Mayor Sanford Biggar to call for help from militia units in Toronto. The riot act is read and crowds are dispersed by force.

5. **1946:** United Steelworkers Local 1005 goes on strike against Stelco, seeking union recognition and a first collective agreement. Demanding higher wages and the establishment of a grievance and seniority procedure, about 12,000 steelworkers spend 80 days on the picket line. However, as many as 1,500 workers, foremen and superintendents stay in the plant and violent clashes result when the company attempts to move steel out on a railway train.

Lakeport Brewery

Most beer drinkers in the country are familiar with the phrase 24 for $24. It was that phrase coined by Teresa Cascioli of Hamilton that helped provide Canada's beer lovers with cheaper prices and helped turn around a small, almost bankrupt brewery in Hamilton.

A native of Hamilton, McMaster graduate and a former manager of finance and administration for the City of Hamilton, Cascioli was recruited in 1999 to take over Lakeport Brewery. At the time, the brewery was in bankruptcy protection. The company was saddled with an inefficient plant, poor reporting systems, and inadequate financing.

She started off by producing branded alcoholic drinks for other companies and producing a line of generic beers. Then, in 2002, she decided to sell Lakeport Honey Lager for a dollar a bottle and came up with the familiar marketing phrase. Part of her decision was influenced by the significant unused capacity of her plant and her knowledge that there was room for a price decrease.

If no one responded to a price decrease, shares would goes up. However, the variance between the mainstream brands and Lakeport was huge. The large brewers were quick to respond to the challenge but as Cascioli stated in the Globe and Mail, "we are a value producer of beer. We make great quality beer and we offer it at $5-10 less than the mainstream brands all year long. We are on sale 365 days of the year."

As the result of her marketing message, Lakeport increased to become Ontario's third largest brewery with 11 percent of the market. Lakeport Honey is the leading honey beer in Ontario and the only honey beer on the beer store's top 10 list. Lakeport Pilsener is also one of the top 10 and their light beer is the fastest growing light beer.

Brewing giant Labatt's recently bought out Lakeport for a reputed $200 million dollars and it is estimated that Cascioli earned $40 million on the deal. In 2007, she donated one million dollars to her alma mater to help educate future entrepreneurs.

POVERTY

- Percentage of persons defined by Statistics Canada as "low income" after taxes in Hamilton in 2006: 14.0
- Percentage of persons defined by Statistics Canada as "low income" after taxes in Ontario in 2006: 11.1
- Number of social assistance beneficiaries in Hamilton in 2006: 23,309
- Number of social assistance beneficiaries in Hamilton in 1999: 25,798
- Consumer bankruptcies in Hamilton in 2006: 1,270
- Consumer bankruptcies in Hamilton in 1999: 1,508

Take 5 TERESA CASCIOLI'S FIVE MANAGEMENT LESSONS

Teresa Cascioli is a former city hall bureaucrat turned entrepreneur who grew Hamilton-based Lakeport Brewing into Ontario's third largest brewer and made the slogan '24 for $24' famous. After selling out to Labatt's, she became a philanthropist and set up her own charitable foundation.

1. Be passionate and work hard.
2. Listen to your employees. Their insights can give you a competitive advantage.
3. Partner well. Surround yourself with good advisors (lawyers, bankers, accountants), and don't nickel and dime them.
4. When you think you've done well, forget it. Don't rest on your laurels or do things just to win awards.
5. Whenever you're in front of a microphone, sell, sell, sell.

> "Entrepreneurs are not always born with the desire to lead. Education is the key to developing essential entrepreneurial skills. Entrepreneurs are found in all fields and disciplines in organizations of any size at any level within an organization. They are professionals who, through their ability to manage risk, can take an organization to a new level. Entrepreneurs are focused and hard working out-of-the-box-thinkers who take risks no one else has tried."
>
> **– Teresa Cascioli on her donation to McMaster University of $1 million dollars to help budding entrepreneurs studying at that school.**

HAMILTON'S POOREST NEIGHBORHOODS

According to the Conference Board of Canada, the lowest taxable incomes are in the downtown and "old sections" of Hamilton at an average of $30,000 per year. The wealthiest areas are Ancaster ($53,300), Flamborough ($46,500) and Dundas ($45,700).

GIMME SHELTER

The average Canadian household's expenditure on shelter in 2006 was $12,986. Average annual household expenditure on shelter in selected Canadian metropolitan areas (2006):

- Toronto: $17,049
- Calgary: $16,794
- Vancouver: $15,800
- Hamilton: $15,163
- Halifax: $12,239
- Winnipeg: $11,271
- Montreal: $11,121

Did you know...

that 27 percent of Hamiltonians live alone, and 31 percent live in 2-person households?

Union Movement

As Hamilton established itself as a leading industrial centre through the mid-19th century, the city's workers found themselves employed in harsh, often dangerous and poor-paying factory jobs. As early as 1864, there were about 2,300 factory workers in the city, toiling for at least 12 hours a day, for poverty wages.

Through the 1860s, skilled workers began to form trade unions, most organized along craft lines, and by 1864, Hamilton boasted a local Trades Association, which was the first of its kind in Canada.

Lobbying for a nine-hour working day and better working conditions in 1872, the city's trade unionists united to lead the Nine-Hour Movement that spread to communities across Southern Ontario and into Quebec. To support their demands, about 1,500 Hamilton workers launched a general strike on May 15, and marched through the city's streets.

Although the strike shut down most of the city's businesses, strikers were gradually forced back to work as employers resisted their demands. By 1903, the city had 59 labour organizations. Trade unionists also began making their voices heard politically, and in the 1919 provincial election Hamilton elected Independent Labour Party members in all three Hamilton ridings.

Workers continued to organize throughout the 1920s and '30s, but efforts were stymied by high unemployment and often rough retribution against union and pro union workers. When government legislation introduced in 1944 gave workers the right to organize, Local 1005 of the United Steelworkers was certified to represent Stelco workers. Two years later, following a heated and confrontational 80-day strike, the steelworkers earned recognition of their union and established their first collective agreement.

Employees with Firestone, Westinghouse and the Hamilton Spectator also took to the picket line that summer, as collective bargaining spread across the country. By building on those earliest contracts over the following decades, unions made continued gains in wages, benefits and job security, eventually providing a middle-class living to Hamilton's thousands of factory workers.

The political force of the labour movement also continues to be felt in Hamilton, where NDP candidates have frequently represented the city at both the provincial and federal levels.

BUYING A HOUSE

As of October 2007, the average house price in Hamilton was $294,625, up ten percent from the year before. Nationally, the average price of buying a home was $317,619. Here's how some other major cities stack up:

- Vancouver $531,000
- Toronto $354,000
- Calgary $376,000
- Ottawa $261,000
- Montreal $210,000
- Halifax $197,000
- Fredericton $130,000
- Regina $117,000

Sources: Canadian Real Estate Association; Living in Canada.

Take 5 FIVE MOST EXPENSIVE HOMES
LISTED IN 2007

1. **Ancaster, Tiffany Falls area, $2.7 million:** five bedrooms, five full bathrooms and one partial; 10,000 sq ft.
2. **18 Turner Avenue, $2.375 million:** on a dead-end street, designed by William Souter and built in 1932; living room features leaded windows with stained glass crests and has the original solarium off it.
3. **546 Sulphur Springs Road, Ancaster, $1.995 million:** a four acre lot with 4,600 sq ft; barrel ceilings with hand painted accents in the living and dining rooms.
4. **496 Wilson Street East, Ancaster, $1.795 million:** century home on 1.7 acres with six bedrooms, four full baths and one partial.
5. **12 Ravenscliffe Avenue, Hamilton, $1.69 million:** built in 1908, seven bedrooms, six bathrooms, six fireplaces, with a basement media room, exercise room, billiard room with the original table, oak flooring and a bar with an expansive wine cellar.

Source: Hamilton Spectator.

Did you know...

that according to a study done by Re/Max Realty, the average price of a house in Hamilton/Burlington rose by 77 percent between 1997 and 2007? During that period, the number of houses that sold for more than $500,000 increased from 39 in 1997 to 529 in 2007.

RENTING

- Percentage of Hamiltonians who rent: 31.7
- Average vacancy rate in Hamilton: 3.5 percent

Rents In Selected Metro Areas:

City	1 bedroom	2 bedrooms
Toronto	$900	$1,061
Calgary	$897	$1089
Vancouver	$788	$1,004
Edmonton	$784	$958
Ottawa	$760	$866
Hamilton	$666	$824
Montreal	$581	$647

Source: Canada Mortgage and Housing Corporation.

THE HAMILTON COMMUTE

The average Canadian spends nearly 12 full days each year traveling between home and work, which works out to approximately 63 minutes a day. The Toronto commute, the longest in Canada, is 80 minutes a day. The Hamilton commute is less, coming in at 65 minutes.

Did you know...

that in Hamilton, the west end was the highest priced area with average house prices of $227,590, followed by the Mountain at $221,448, the east end at $169,149 and the centre city at $130,719?

Take 5 TOP FIVE EMPLOYERS

1. **City of Hamilton:** 9,000 employees
2. **Hamilton Health Science Corporation:** 8,680 employees
3. **McMaster University:** 7,500 employees
4. **ArcelorMittal Dofasco:** 7,400 employees
5. **U.S. Steel Canada:** 2,200 employees

HOW WE GET TO WORK

- 83.4 percent drive
- 9.3 percent use public transit
- 6.3 percent walk or bicycle
- 0.9 percent find other means

Source: Statistics Canada.

NO PARKING

The *Hamilton Spectator* described parking in Hamilton as among the cheapest in Canada with hourly rates for parking on main streets at only a dollar an hour. Some of the municipal car parks in the city charge as little as $3 for all day parking. The average hourly rate for all streets is 61 cents an hour. This compares to $1.46 average in Toronto and $2.50 in Ottawa.

- Median cost of monthly parking in Hamilton: $120
- Median cost in Edmonton: $140
- Median cost in Vancouver: $194
- Median cost in Montreal: $259
- Median cost in Toronto: $300
- Median cost in Calgary: $350
- Canadian average: $194.51

They Said It

> "Even good suppliers, agents and employees can get complacent or, heaven forbid, incompetent. My biggest career mistake was to not have an exit strategy or expiry date on contracts and commitments."
>
> **– Ron Foxcroft, inventor of the Fox 40 whistle and head of Fluke Transportation.**

EMPLOYMENT BY SECTOR (PERCENTAGE OF TOTAL EMPLOYMENT)

- Management: 8.9
- Business, finance and administration: 16.5
- Health: 6.6
- Sales and service: 24.7
- Processing and manufacturing: 7.4
- Natural and applied science: 5.4
- Trades, transport and equipment operators: 17.1
- Other: 13.4

Source: Statistics Canada.

UNEMPLOYMENT

- Number of people employed (2008): 382,000
- Hamilton's unemployment rate (2008): 5.8 percent
- Canada's unemployment rate (2008): 6.1 percent

GENDER GAP

- Percentage of men who work: 70.2
- Percentage of women who work: 59.5
- Median income of men age 15 and older in Hamilton in 2006: $36,857
- Median income of women in 2006: $22,473 (women earn 57.8 percent of men's earnings)

Source: Statistics Canada.

HOME-BASED WORK
A total of 13,600 workers in 2006 were home-based; an increase of 10.5 percent from 2001, a trend that is likely to continue. Of the total work force, 5.5 percent worked at home in Hamilton compared to 7.1 percent in the rest of the province.

SMALL BUSINESS (LESS THAN 50 EMPLOYEES)
- Total number of small businesses: 7,588
- Small businesses as a percentage of total businesses: 97
- Number of small businesses with 1-4 employees: 4,355 (59.2 percent of all small businesses)
- 5-9 employees: 1,673 (22.7 percent)
- 10-19 employees: 862 (11.7 percent)
- 20-49 employees: 470 (6.4 percent)

Source: City of Hamilton.

DOWNTOWN OFFICES
The Hamilton office vacancy rate was 21 percent in 2007 and the cost of 'Class A' downtown office space $15-24 gross per square foot.

BUILDING PERMITS

PERMITS	2007	Percent Change From '06
Residential	$395,335,459	- 3
Commercial	$126,391,480	+ 17
Industrial	$63,337,586	- 12
Institutional	$210,207,720	+ 147
Miscellaneous	$6,446,743	- 24
Total	$801,719,318	+ 17

Did you know...

that in September 2007, the U.S. based Site Selection Magazine rated the City of Hamilton one of the top five best locations in Canada for investing and growing a businesses?

TRANSPORTATION INFRASTRUCTURE
Air

John C Munro Hamilton International airport is increasingly being seen by travelers as an alternative to Toronto's Pearson International. For passengers, it offers competitive passenger carrier service, low airport fees, quick aircraft turn-around, no congestion and convenient low cost parking. Passenger numbers increased 26 percent from 2002-2006 to 662,855. In addition to Westjet and Air Canada, passengers can fly to many cities in the UK and Ireland via Flyglobespan.

Hamilton International is also Canada's largest courier and cargo airport generating more cargo flights than any other airport in Canada. Its 24 hour — 365 day cargo operation and strategic geographic location make it Canada's largest integrated courier airport and its link to the major cargo hubs of the world. Cargojet, Purolator, UPS and DHL each have substantial sort and cross-dock facilities at the airport.

Cargojet is also expanding its operations at the airport by doubling the size of its maintenance hanger, adding two new 767s and one 757 to its fleet of 14 smaller 727s and add 50 to 100 new staff over the next 18 months. Cargo service to Europe will begin in the fall of 2008.

Did you know...

that the John C Munro Hamilton International Airport was named after one of the city's political giants? John C. Munro was born in Hamilton in 1931, and attended Westdale Collegiate, McMaster University, the University of Western Ontario, and Osgoode Hall Law School. In the early 1980s, he secured over $55 million in federal investment for what was then known as the Mount Hope Airport.

Sea

Located at the center of Ontario's Golden Horseshoe, the port is perhaps the most important piece of the infrastructure of the city and surrounding region. It is the busiest commercial Canadian port on the Great Lakes, and one of the busiest in the country. In 2007, almost 12 million tonnes of material moved through the port. (By comparison, the Port of Montreal —the largest in the country — moved 20 million tonnes.) Total vessels arriving at the port reached the 700 mark for the third consecutive year.

Road

Hamilton sits on the mid point of the Queen Elizabeth Way — a major highway running from Metropolitan Toronto to the U.S. border at both Niagara Falls and Buffalo. It also sits at the end of the electronic expressway, the 407, which takes vehicles to the North End of Toronto and across to the markets in Eastern Ontario.

Via the 403, Hamilton exporters have easy access to highway 401 — the Canadian link to the NAFTA super highway connecting Ontario with the I-75 serving Michigan, Ohio, Kentucky, Tennessee, Georgia and Florida and the I-90 connections to the eastern seaboard. With the U. S. border only an hour's drive, Hamilton is within half a day's drive of key major urban markets in the United States.

On November 17, 2007, the Red Hill Expressway opened. This road contributes to an effective transportation system and it opens many of the growing new industrial areas in Glanbrook and the airport to easier connections to the QEW and the U.S. market.

Did you know...

that ArcelorMittal Dofasco is pumping $119 million into its Hamilton operations in a bid to boost steel production by 20 per cent?

Take 5 TOP FIVE FARM CROPS
(2006)

1. Greenhouse products	$44.6 million
2. Poultry and egg	$40.2 million
3. Nursery products and sod	$33.7 million
4. Wheat grain and oilseed	$19.5 million
5. Dairy	$14.2 million

FARMIN' IN THE CITY

Believe it or not, agriculture is a booming one billion dollars per year industry even within the city limits of Hamilton. Over 140,000 acres — 60 percent of Hamilton's total area — is farmed and because of the physiography, soils and climate, the city is able to grow substantial tender fruit crops that cannot be grown in many other parts of the country. The agricultural industry is home to about 1,500 farms and employs over 4,100 people.

TOURISM

Because Hamilton is so easily accessible via road, water, air, and rail, the city tends to welcome between three and four million visitors per year, with visitors spending approximately $186 million annually. The industry provides employment to almost 2,400 Hamiltonians.

Source: Tourism Hamilton.

Did you know...

that 61 percent of Hamilton's farms are under 130 acres?

GETTING BETTER AND BETTER

The Downtown Hamilton Business Improvement Area was formed in 1982 by several merchants and business owners. It is a non-profit organization that oversees the improvement, beautification and maintenance of municipally-owned land, buildings and structures. The organization currently has 453 members and 173 property owners who are taxed a special levy over and above their taxes to help fund the activities of the BIA.

Did you know...

that one of the world's largest manufacturers of juggling supplies making a quarter of a million balls a year is located in Hamilton? The company, Higgins Brothers Inc and originally known as Great Canadian Balls, is coming out with a line of Cirque du Soleil products.

Weblinks

Hamilton Economic Development
www.investinhamilton.ca
Hamilton wants you to 'invest in Hamilton,' and here, they tell you everything you need to know about the city, from business services to incentives & programs, to what it's like to live here.

Hamilton Business Directory
www.hamiltondirectory.ca
Start your business search here.

Downtown Hamilton
www.downtownhamilton.org
Maps, virtual tour, membership directory, hot properties, downtown links, government programs, events, and more.

TOUCHDOWN

THE CANADIAN FOOTBALL
HALL OF FAME

Culture

To many, Hamilton is yet another fading North American rustbelt city. The truth of the matter is that great cities are measured in part by their resilience and their ability to embrace change and contradiction. Hamilton has weathered the economic change from a manufacturing economy to a knowledge-based economy. It embraces its blue collar identity, while recognizing the importance of learning institutions such as McMaster University.

It is no accident that Ronnie Hawkins played his first gig in Hamilton, the Hamilton bar patrons prompting the singer to think he'd gone to rock and roll heaven. This is still a raucous Steel Town, but with a twist. The galleries seem less contrived than that other big city down the road. Somehow or another, events like the James Street North Art Crawl, where gallery goers jump from one gallery and cafe to another, seem more real and authentic.

Downtown Hamilton is enjoying a bit of renaissance. New theatre troupes have emerged. Opera Hamilton is the fourth largest opera company in the country and the Hamilton Philharmonic Orchestra has now been in business in one form or another for 125 years.

Hamilton has also produced more than its fair share of talent that has gone on to the world stage. Martin Short, Daniel Lanois, Eugene Levy, Ivan Reitman, Tom Wilson, Stan Rogers, Steve Smith, and

Karen Kain are just a few and are sure to be joined by many more in the years to come.

ARTISTS
- Number of artists in Hamilton: 1,700
- Number of artists in Canada: 131,000
- Hamilton's artists' average earnings: $21,600
- Gap between artists' earnings and overall workforce average: 35 percent

HAMILTON HAS
- 105 actors
- 220 artisans and craft persons
- 50 conductors, composers and arrangers
- 140 dancers
- 455 musicians and singers
- 175 painters, sculptors and other visual artists
- 195 producers, directors and choreographers
- 260 writers
- 100 not classified

Source: Canada Council for the Arts.

ALL IN A YEAR'S WORK (AVERAGE SALARY IN ONTARIO)
- Writers: $35,798
- Producers, directors, and choreographers: $45,752
- Actors: $24,142
- Artisans: $16,798
- Painters and sculptors: $24,955
- Dancers: $14,945
- Musicians and singers: $18,353

THAT'S AN ORDER
- Hamilton's recipients of the Order of Canada: 29

- Members of the Order: 8
- Officers of the Order: 19
- Companions of the Order: 2

Source: Governor General of Canada.

RECOGNITION OF THE ARTS

In 2006, Hamilton received $1,157,950 from the Canadian Council for the Arts. That comes to $681.15 for each of the 1,700 artists in the city. Literary and publishing received $120,900 of the total while art got $407,400, music got $397,150 and the theatre received $232,500.

HAMILTON ARTS AWARDS

The City of Hamilton Arts Awards are given every November to practicing artists in the Hamilton area to recognize their significant contributions in their chosen discipline. The Arts Awards are comprised of five awards for work in the areas of literature, visual art, theatre, dance and music. The following are the 2007 winners; actor Tom Mackan, poet Jeff Seffinga, singer John Fanning, photographer Dennis McGreal, and conductor Boris Brott.

Previous winners include:

Herb Barrett, Literature; Wesley Bates, Visual Arts; Jessie L. Beattie, Literature; Clyde Brooks, Literature; Boris Brott, Lifetime Achievement; Trevor Cole, Literature; Pat Dawson, Theatre; Spencer Dunmore, Literature; John Fanning, Music; Emily Dutton & Marion Farnan, Visual Arts; Conrad Furey, Visual Arts; Robert Gibb, Theatre; Paul Gordon, Dance; V. Jane Gordon, Visual Arts; Christine Hamilton, Theatre; Trevor Hodgson, Visual Arts; Jude Johnson, Music; Bryce Kanbara, Visual Arts; Lois Laxton, Lifetime Achievement; Paul Lisson, Literature & Visual Arts; Thomas Reid MacDonald, Visual Arts; Tom Mackan, Theatre; Dennis McGreal, Visual Arts; Glen A. Mallory, Music; Robert Mason, Visual Arts;

Archibald C.R. Mullock, Theatre; Pam Norman, Visual Arts; Alan Oddy, Visual Arts; Dani Podetz, Theatre; Bill Powell, The Arts; Rachel Preston, Literature; Max Reimer, Theatre; Stan Rogers, Music; Gary Santucci, Music; Jeff Seffinga, Literature; Jame Strecker, Literature; Cheryl Takacs, Visual Arts; Elsie E. Thomson, Theatre; Mary Toplack, Visual Arts; Tom Wilson, Music; Vitek Wincza, Dance; Jackie Washington, Music; Russ Weil, Music; Mike Woods, Music and Lou Zamprogna, Lifetime Achievement.

LITERATURE
Number of Hamilton writers nominated for the Governor General's Award: 1 nominated twice (David MacFadden)
- Number who have won the award: none
- Number of Hamilton writers nominated for the Scotiabank Giller Award: 1
- Number who have won the award: none

PERFORMING ARTS
In Hamilton, you can bank on seeing live theatric performances almost every single day of the year. Theatre Aquarius is probably the best-known gem as well as the third largest regional theatre in the province; their motto is to "tell the stories of heart, humour and humanity that shape and describe our experiences in Hamilton, Ontario and Canada."

The Ronald V Joyce Centre for the Performing Arts has a reputation for its outstanding acoustics, while the Players Guild of Hamilton has been around since 1875, raising money earned from performances

Did you know...

that the Tower Poetry Society founded in 1951 is the oldest poetry collective in Canada and one of the oldest in North America? They publish two issues of their poetry every year and meet monthly.

Take 5 FIVE HAMILTON WRITERS

1. **Jean Rae Baxter** returned to Hamilton, her hometown, in 1996 after a career teaching English in the Kingston area. Described as a literary Jekyll and Hyde by one reviewer, she writes crime fiction for adults and historical fiction for teens. *A Twist of Malice*, her first collection of short stories, was published to critical acclaim in 2005. The *Way Lies North*, her young adult novel about a teenage girl during the American Revolution, was published in 2007.

2. Award-winning Dundas author **Gillian Chan** has written several books for children and teens. A 2006 contestant on the TV quiz show *Jeopardy*, Chan was nominated for a Governor-General's Award for *Glory Days and Other Stories*, published in 1996. In 2004 she published a book for Scholastic's Dear Canada series, *An Ocean Apart: The Gold Mountain Diary of Chin Mei-ling*.

3. A Hamilton-based journalist for several national magazines, **Trevor William Cole** published his first two novels *Norman Bray, in the Performance of His Life* and *The Fearsome Particles* in 2004 and 2006, respectively. Both were nominated for Governor-General's Awards.

4. Born in Hamilton, **David Macfarlane** is an award-winning journalist and newspaper columnist. His first novel, *Summer Gone*, was shortlisted for the Giller Prize in 1999 and won the Books in Canada First Novel Award.

5. Poet, author and cabinetmaker **John Terpstra** won the Bressani Award for his 1987 collection of poetry *Forty Days & Forty Nights*. He was also nominated for the Governor-General's award for poetry for a 2003 collection, *Disarmament*. One of his best known works is *The Boys, Or, Waiting for the Electrician's Daughter*, a 2005 memoir about his wife's three brothers, all of whom lived with muscular dystrophy.

for local charities. Hamilton Theatre Inc. has produced favourite performances such as Grease, Annie, Cabaret, Urinetown — the Musical, and Little Shop of Horrors.

Smaller theatres abound all over the city. Some of these include the Dundas Little Theatre, the Binbrook Little Theatre, the Great Big Theatre Company (for children), The Geritol Follies, and Theatre Ancaster.

Take 5 FIVE PLACES TO SEE ART

1. **The Art Gallery of Hamilton** was founded in 1914 and is, today, the third largest art gallery in Ontario with over 9,000 pieces. Its collection includes historical Canadian and European art and contemporary works. Exhibitions change three times a year and the visitors can enjoy the cafe if they find they spend so much time that they work up an appetite.

2. **Irving Zucker Sculpture Court** is adjacent to the art gallery but can be visited by passersby walking along Main St. and by downtown office workers as a pleasant spot for lunch. In 1990, philanthropist Irving Zucker donated major works to the Art Gallery by Canadian painter Jean-Paul Riopelle and British sculptor Lynn Chadwick. Until his death in 2002, Zucker donated many works to the gallery including a considerable number of sculptures. As part of the renovation of the gallery, the sculpture garden was made more visible from the street so that it could be enjoyed by all.

3. **McMaster Museum of Art** is on the campus of the university. Works at the museum emphasize the relationship between the teaching of art, art history and other subject areas (especially within the Humanities) as well as broader concerns such as learning, research and public enjoyment. Within this context, three areas have been singled out for development -- Canadian art, early 20th

LET'S CELEBRATE!

Hamilton is a city that likes to celebrate. Each season holds different festivals some, of course, larger than others. The month of August, for example, hosts the internationally-known Mustard Festival. (The city is one of the world's largest millers of dry mustard.)

Also in August is the Cactus Festival. Needing an excuse for a sum-

century German Expressionist art and modern and contemporary European art.

4. **James St. North Arts Crawl** is an opportunity for people to economize their time while visiting many of the new, small and unique art studios in this area. The crawl takes place on the second Friday night of each month and the galleries co-ordinate their openings to coincide with the event. For those who wish to explore galleries in other parts of the city, a bus tour is also available on the second Friday of each month. Tickets can be arranged through Arts Hamilton. Their website lists all the small galleries in the city and the list is impressive.

5. **The Cottage Studio** is one of the more unique art studios/galleries to be found anywhere. Originally begun in 1993 as a place for those with serious mental illnesses to pursue their art interests, it has grown over the years and provides lessons and gallery space for some very talented people who just happen to have serious mental illnesses. With financial support from the Ontario Trillium Fund, they moved out of the basement of St. Paul's Presbyterian Church on James St. S and into a newly renovated historical cottage on the church grounds. Works by the artists are on display and for sale and examples can be found on their website along with opening hours.

Take 5   FIVE PERFORMERS
FROM HAMILTON

1. **Karen Kain**; prima ballerina and former principal dancer with the National Ballet of Canada.
2. **Wendy Crewson**; actress, producer.
3. **Eugene Levy**; writer, producer, director, comic actor.
4. **Martin Short**; actor, comedian.
5. **Gema Zamprogna**; actor, dancer.

mer party, the town residents discovered that the Ben Veldhuis Cactus greenhouses were internationally recognized for their cacti. The greenhouse is no longer but the citizens still "party on" to the cactus theme. Nearing the end of the month, residents gather to celebrate the peach harvest in and around local orchards with the Winona Peach Festival.

Other summer festivals include the Festival of Friends, the second largest musical festival in the country. Since 1975, headliners like Valdy, Don McLean, Randy Bachman and Eric Burdon and the Animals have played here.

There is also the Ice Cream Festival at Westfield Village, the Hamilton Mardigras Carnival, and Hamilton's Fringe Festival. If you're not around for the lazy days of summer, fret not; you can always catch festivals like the Locke Street Festival, Festitalia, the Ancaster Fair, the Mum Show, and 'Twas the Night Before Christmas.

They Said It

> "I was raised in Hamilton and am planning to return permanently this coming spring … Hamilton's downtown is the only authentic downtown in Ontario. It has the gritty charm and feel of an authentic urban area with density, independent commerce, and pioneering artists. It's the least pretentious city I've ever lived in."
>
> **– Tim Jacobs, Kelowna BC, quoted in the *Hamilton Spectator*.**

MUSEUMS

- Battlefield House Museum and Park: A National Historic Site complete with costumed interpreters.
- Canadian Football Hall of Fame and Museum: Exhibits that showcase every aspect of Canadian football.
- Canadian Warplane Heritage Museum: Over 40 World War II aircrafts on display.
- Dundas Museum: Take a walk back through the history of Dundas.

Take 5 HAMILTON CRAFTSPEOPLE

A large number of artisans and crafts people in the Hamilton area produce outstanding work. A brief sampler includes:

1. **Lorraine Roy**, an award-winning textile artist who creates exquisite fabric wall hangings using what she calls "collage with nets." The effect is intensely colorful, three dimensional images reminiscent of pointillism.

2. **Shirley Elford** is an internationally recognized glass blower and artist noted for her exquisite glass sculptures. Many are presentation pieces, including the new Juno award which she designed for the Canadian Academy of Recording Arts and Sciences in 2000.

3. **Lucy Slykerman** produces hand-woven cloth, including fine silk, using a special dyeing technique that allows her to "paint" the stunning fabric.

4. **Colleen O'Reilly-Lafferty** is a world-class potter renowned for her unusual porcelain tableware, some of which has been presented to heads-of-state visiting Canada.

5. **Debi Keir-Nicholson** runs Beads of Colour, a studio and shop which she stocks with beads she has sourced from all over the world. Her unique jewellery designs often incorporate handmade beads from exotic locales.

- Dundurn Castle: The former home of Sir Allan Napier MacNab will help you discover mid-19th-century Hamilton.
- Erland Lee Museum: A Gothic Revival farmhouse; home of the original Women's Institutes.
- Fieldcote Memorial Park & Museum: A cultural heritage centre.
- Griffin House: A testament of the Black men and women's bravery and determination.
- Hamilton's Children Museum: Hands on activities for both children and their parents.
- Hamilton Military Museum: Focuses on the War of 1812, the Boer War, and WWI.
- Hamilton Museum of Steam and Technology: Two 70-ton steam engines are the star attractions here.
- HMCS Haida: Stroll the decks of the last Tribal Class destroyer in the world.
- Parks Canada Discovery Centre: Historic places and natural spaces.
- Whitehern Historic House & Garden: A National Historic Site.

FILM

The great irony of the film industry in Toronto is that it has made a substantial part of its living doubling as an American city. Today Hamilton sometimes earns its keep doubling as Toronto. With 106 productions in 2007, the film business is no a longer a fringe industry in the city, it is an industry.

FILM AND TV PRODUCTIONS IN HAMILTON (ECONOMIC IMPACT)

2007: 106 productions ($12 million)
2006: 94 productions ($15 million)
2005: 90 productions ($15.6 million)
2004: 48 productions ($10.5 million)
2003: 45 productions ($8 million)

Source: Invest in Hamilton.

Bio MARTY

Martin Short was born in Hamilton in 1950 and got his BA in Sociology in 1972 from McMaster University. His mother, Olive Short, was a former child prodigy. She played classical violin with the Hamilton Philharmonic and in the process became the first female concertmaster in North America. His father on the other hand arrived in Canada from Ireland as a stowaway, rising eventually to becoming an executive at Stelco.

His classmates at McMaster were Eugene Levy and Dave Thomas. Upon graduation, he appeared in the 1972 Toronto production of *Godspell* with Levy, Gilda Radner, Victor Garber and Andrea Martin. In 1977, Short joined the improv troupe The Second City, something which would launch him on the international stage. The ground breaking television show SCTV followed, first in Canada, then the U.S. It was here Short honed his sense of parody and developed characters as Brock Linehan (based on film critic Brian Linehan). It is no surprise that Saturday Night Live came calling. Characters like Ed Grimley, Natha Thurm and Jackie Rogers, Jr. are now part of the American landscape.

He made his Broadway debut opposite Bernadette Peters in the 1993 musical adaptation of *The Goodbye Girl*, for which he received a Tony nomination. He won a Tony in 1999 for his appearance in the revival of *Little Me*. In 2006 he performed in and co-wrote the autobiographical Broadway musical, "Martin Short: Fame Becomes Me," a twisted take on the trend of soul-baring, one-person shows.

Short also developed other television vehicles. The Martin Short Show appeared in 1994 and in 2001 he launched what is probably his best-known character, Jiminy Glick, in Primetime Glick.

Shorts film work includes the *Three Amigos, Innerspace, Three Fugitives*, and *The Big Picture*. In 1994, he became a recipient of the Order of Canada. Short has spoken often and fondly of the influence of Hamilton on who he has become. He would like to be remembered, he has said "as someone who really seemed to appreciate the importance of having a good time."

Take 5 FIVE FILMS
SHOT IN HAMILTON

1. *Hairspray* with John Travolta
2. *The Hulk* with Edward Norton, Liv Tyler, and William Hurt
3. *Against the Ropes* with Meg Ryan
4. *Man of the Year* with Robin Williams
5. *The Long Kiss Goodbye* with Geena Davis and Samuel L. Jackson

MUSIC

Hamilton has produced a disproportionate number of musicians that have gone on to bigger stages. That includes everybody from folkster Stan Rogers to blues legends Jackie Washington and King Biscuit Boy to "Painted Lady" penman Ian Thomas and Neil Peart from the rock group Rush. In the 1970s and 80s Hamilton was an important centre of punk rock, producing acts such as Forgotten Rebels and The Dik van Dykes.

Current indie and mainstream names include singer-songwriters Sarah Harmer, Tomi Swick, Mayor McCa and Wax Mannequin, Canadian Idol Brian Melo, and rockers Tom Wilson, Cities in the Dust, A Northern Chorus and brothers Christian and Jagori Tanna from I Mother Earth.

Did you know...

that 2007's Canadian Idol winner, 24-year-old Brian Melo from Hamilton, used to earn his living as a construction worker?

Bio **BORIS BROTT**

Boris Brott is a one-man tour de force. When he arrived in Hamilton in 1969 at the age of 25, he was very much a man on the rise. He had literally been performing since he was three years old. His father was a concert violinist in Montreal and quickly had him studying both there and in Europe.

At 14, Brott won first prize at the 1958 Pan-American conducting competition and the next year he founded the Philharmonic Youth Orchestra of Montreal. Before he arrived in Hamilton, he served as the assistant conductor of Walter Susskind with the Toronto Symphony Orchestra and as conductor of the Northern Sinfonia at Newcastle-on-Tyne. When he moved back to Canada, it was to become the first music coordinator at Lakehead University.

When Brott arrived in Hamilton to head the Hamilton Philharmonic Orchestra, it was largely an amateur organization held together by a small but loyal membership. Under Brott, the subscriber base grew to 16,000 and the largely amateur group grew into one of the country's most important professional orchestras.

The Brott Music Festival, which began as a festival in Hamilton in 1988 to offer training to young musicians and to help keep the skills of professional musicians sharp during the slow season, has grown into a 20 week-long series of spring, summer and autumn festivals in Hamilton, Toronto and the Muskoka region.

Brott is an international superstar who has chosen to make Hamilton his hometown and stomping grounds. Brott's contributions to the community are many but the most important contribution is that he has made the Hamilton Philharmonic Orchestra a relevant and integral part of Hamilton's cultural community. In 2007, the City of Hamilton recognized him for that contribution with its Lifetime Achievement Arts Award.

Brott continues to keep a busy schedule. He is the conductor and music director of the New West Symphony in California, the McGill Chamber Orchestra in Montreal, the National Academy Orchestra of Canada and Principal Youth and Family Conductor of the National Arts Center of Canada. He also continues to be the artistic director of the Brott Musical Festivals. It is also no surprise that Brott's enthusiasm for life and music has resonated on Wall and Bay streets. He currently gives more than 35 talks annually around the world for Fortune 500 companies.

They Said It

"It is, well, pretty fantastic."
– **David Estok commenting on Hamilton's homegrown musical talent.**

A number of recording studios reside in Hamilton, the most famous of which is the Grant Avenue Recording Studio started over 25 years ago by Daniel Lanois. Another notable studio is the Sonic Unyon label, one of the country's most successful indie record labels and distributors.

The city is passionate about music. The country's Juno Awards have been held in Hamilton five times since 1995. That's the most for any city outside of Toronto.

SINGING CLASSICAL AND CHOIRS

Opera Hamilton is the fourth largest opera company in Canada and includes the audience favourite, POPERA, a seasonal 'highlights' concert. The Hamilton Philharmonic Orchestra has been performing for over 125 years and prides itself on cultivating music appreciation and education with the city.

Since 1977, the Hamilton-based Canadian Orpheus Male Chorus has sung all over the world including Westminster Abbey and the Royal Albert Hall in London. The Bach Elgar choir has been singing everything from classics to Broadway tunes since 1905 and is the second oldest choral organization in the country.

Did you know...

that the Bach Elgar Choir was first established in 1905 as the Elgar Choir? In 1910, the choir attained international recognition by giving the North American premiere performance of Verdi's Requiem with the Toronto Symphony Orchestra.

Grant Street

Daniel Lanois has been called one of the world's most important record producers by *Rolling Stone*. Although he was born in Hull, Quebec, his mother moved him and his three siblings to Hamilton when he was just ten. His mother sang while his father and grandfather played fiddle. It wasn't long before young Daniel learned guitar and began playing in local groups.

Very early on, Lanois was always playing with effects. He started playing with echo effects on his Sony reel to reel in a basement studio that he and his brother built. For sound insulation, they covered the walls with 300 egg cartons they bought from Turkstra's Eggs on Guelph Rd. In his film, *Here is What Is*, he says, "I found that because of the size of my hands I could reach a lot of faders at once. And because of my musicality, I could move the faders in a musical way. So I don't see the console as a piece of technological equipment, particularly. I see it as an instrument, as a musical instrument."

Lanois, of course, would outgrow the family basement. He fixed up an old house on Grant Avenue and launched Grant Avenue Studio which would become famous well beyond the boundaries of Hamilton. In 1980, Lanois caught a break that launched his career. A group he recorded, Time Twins, sent out a demo one of which was heard by British producer Brian Eno. Eno was so impressed with the production that he was on a plane to meet Lanois.

Eno was even more impressed once he met Lanois and invited him to co-produce U2's album *The Unforgettable Fire*. From there he went on to co-produce U2's 1987 Grammy winning album of the year, *The Joshua Tree*. Over the years now he has worked extensively with the likes of Bob Dylan and Emmylou Harris.

He has won Grammys, Junos, been elected to the Canadian Music Hall of Fame, and received an honourary doctorate from McMaster University. In 2005, when Lanois accepted a lifetime achievement honour at the Hamilton Music Awards, a message from U2 was beamed to the presentation at the Dofasco Centre for the Arts. Bono interrupted a concert in Atlanta and in front of 18,000 fans in Atlanta, he told the audience the following: "We want to do a TV broadcast right now to Hamilton in Canada. It is the place where Daniel Lanois grew up. We love Danny boy Lanois and without him we would not be here."

They Said It

"If music be the food of love, then play on. Hamilton may well have more great musicians per capita than doughnut shops."
— **Mary K. Nolan** in the *Hamilton Spectator*.

GET STUFFED

As home to the country's first Tim Horton's, Hamilton can justly lay claim to be the doughnut capital of Canada. It is an unfair title, however, because when it comes to cuisine, the Hammer's almost 500 eateries and bars offer so much more than fried sugar and flour concoctions.

Hamilton is still a working man's town and as a result there is no shortage of restaurants that serve bountiful meals at reasonable prices. Like any large city, Hamilton has the usual chains, but the real delight is in the locally owned pubs, fine dining establishments and the range of ethnic eateries, including Greek, Italian, Indian, Japanese, Thai, German and Middle Eastern.

If you're looking for a view to go with your meal, there are plenty of notable eateries that will take your breath away as you graze; Baranga's on the Beach is just yards away from the shores of Lake Ontario, as is the stunning Edgewater Manor Restaurant. For some famous fish and chips, check out 50s diner Hutch's Dingley Dell, or if you're more in a 'steely' kind of mood, drop by the Old Powerhouse, a typical 19th century industrial building now refurbished with antiques and serving up casual fine food in six dining rooms.

Hamilton's location in the middle of some of the best farmland in

Did you know...

that Boris Brott, who led the Hamilton Philharmonic Orchestra for 21 years and created the Brott Music Festival in Hamilton, was once the assistant of Leonard Bernstein, a world-famous conductor, composer, author and pianist?

Canada, and close to Niagara's world-class vineyards and Great Lakes fisheries, makes it a diner's delight. Many residents are embracing the slow food movement, and food entrepreneurs are taking notice, like restaurants such as the Ancaster Old Mill, Boo's Bistro, the Courtyard, and the Spotted Pig.

Take 5 SHAWN BRUSH'S FIVE GREAT
PLACES TO LISTEN TO LIVE MUSIC

Shawn Brush, known as the Krooked Cowboy, is a local Hamilton singer/songwriter who was described by Bruce Mowat in the *Hamilton Spectator* as having "a dry bittersweet style reminiscent of newgrass picker Norman Blake, or an esoteric version of John Prine." Five of his favourite spots to listen to live music in Hamilton are:

1. **The Casbah** on King St. W. In addition to musicians from outside Hamilton, it is a favourite spot for CD launches by local musicians. And it has good food!

2. **The West Town** on Locke St. provides a venue for many local singers and songwriters.

3. **Slainte**, downtown on an almost invisible side street of Main, is an Irish pub that features both Celtic music and rock and roll. It is in an historic renovated building that once was a horse livery.

4. For edgier hard rock, punk and rock and roll there is **the Underground** on Catharine St. N.

5. **The Coach and Lantern** is a little farther out in Ancaster but it also showcases a lot of local talent. It is another historical stone building. It is the third oldest building in Ancaster and was originally built in the late 1700's but it burnt down and was rebuilt in 1823.

Take 5 KATRINA SIMMONS'
FIVE FAVOURITE DINING SPOTS'

Simmons is the food writer for the *Hamilton Spectator*. She has written about area chefs, their training, likes and preferences for a number of years. She is also a specialist in organic food and the use of local products in the food industry. These five were chosen by her for their character, service, great food, and the fact that they are independent.

1. **Saigon Asian Restaurant** in Westdale for great noodle soups, quick service, and the cleanest washrooms of any of the Asian restaurants in the city. The staff remember their customers too.

2. **Cafe Troy** (Hwy 5 in Troy-now part of Hamilton) for supporting local farmers, its ambiance and beautiful table settings (all pottery made by Donn Zver, next door).

3. **Ancaster Old Mill** supports local farmers and wineries, gets involved in community, encourages staff to explore new trends, and location, location, location.

4. **Dalina's Middle East Cuisine** is a comfortable little place, with real table linen, and the Egyptian owner has been there serving her own creations and some old favorites for more than 20 years.

5. **O Marinero / the Sailor** on James Street North is a family-run Portuguese restaurant; no better place in Hamilton if you like fish. Nothing fancy, just good, hearty fare at a very reasonable price. Bring a healthy appetite.

Toboganning

Because of the Mountain, tobogganing in the city used to be extremely popular in the late 1800s. Hamilton had a few different tobogganing clubs, and they had to limit their memberships to 100 people each because so many more wanted to take part. The Victoria Toboggan and Snowshoe Club, located out of Victoria Avenue South, and the Hamilton Toboggan and Snowshoe Club, based at the corner of Aberdeen and Locke Street South were the most prominent, and each had a large wooden slide used to compete. During the 1887 winter carnival, the slides were opened to the public, and even the *Hamilton Spectator* was there to report the story.

HAMILTON EAT LOCAL

Hamilton Eat Local was formed by Environment Hamilton and other community partners to support programs that encourage Hamiltonians to buy food grown by local farmers, learn to grow their own food and harvest food that would otherwise go to waste. In 2007, Hamilton Eat Local launched the Hamilton and area local food map and directory "Buy local! Buy fresh!"

Did you know...

that there are more Tim Horton's per capita in Hamilton than in any other community in the country?

They Said It

"When you make a mistake [in football], the impact of that mistake runs for at least a season. There's no reboot button in football. You can't change it immediately."

– Bob Young, new owner of the Hamilton Tiger Cats on their losing seasons since he took over.

TASTE THE DOWNTOWN

Every March, there is a food lovers festival called Tastes of Downtown, a walking tour of approximately 20 restaurants, many of them award-winning. It's a win-win-win situation; Hamiltonians get to taste a wide range of dishes, restaurants get to showcase their menus, and all the money raised is donated locally to a good cause. Some restaurants that have participated in previous years are Capri Ristorante, Slainte Irish Pub, Curry Cabana, My-Thai Restaurant, Room Forty One, and Wild Orchid.

Did you know...

that a section of Glennie St. in Hamilton was renamed Pat Quinn Way and in 2005, the local arena in the area was also renamed in Pat Quinn's honour? Quinn was the former coach of four NHL teams and the 2002 Olympic gold medal winning hockey team.

Did you know...

that Toller Cranston was born in Hamilton, Ontario in 1949 and grew up in Kirkland Lake? He was the Canadian national figure skating champion from 1971 to 1976.

Market Day

"From a chicken to a yoke of oxen, from a cherry to a cabbage, from anything to everything ... here you'll find it." That's how Harriet Leland, the wife of the United States consul to Hamilton, described the Farmers' Market in the late 1870s. Leland would still be right today.

Located at 55 York Boulevard, right next to the library and Copps' Coliseum, the Farmers' Market is simply one of the best in Ontario. It was established in 1837 when Andrew "Yankee" Miller and his wife transferred a small parcel of land to the President and Board of Police of the Town of Hamilton. Miller's politics would get him arrested following the Rebellion later that same year and he would return to his native New York. By that time, however, the market at the corner of York and James Streets was thriving.

The Farmers' Market has undergone many changes, starting with a wooden Market Hall completed in 1839 (it also housed a concert stage and city hall). A newer building replaced it in the 1860s and then in the 1880s, when an ornate Victorian brick building was constructed. Following a period of sweeping urban renewal, the market found its present home under the library in 1980.

Today the two levels are completely indoors, with 176 stalls and about 80 vendors, some of whom have been selling there for generations. A visit to the market is a feast for the senses — the smell of fresh fruit and vegetables blend with herbs, home-baked goods and flowers amid a riot of colours. Tuesdays, Thursdays, Fridays and Saturdays, the market is a crossroads, a gathering place for anyone seeking ingredients for cuisine ranging from British to Asian, Portuguese and Caribbean.

DENNINGER'S FINE FOODS OF THE WORLD

For some, it's the lunch counter that is the big draw at Denninger's. But for foodies, the grocery star is about as close to paradise as you can find in Hamilton. It is one of the largest family-owned specialty food companies with retail locations in Oakville, Burlington, Stoney Creek and Hamilton.

Tiger Cats

The Hamilton Tiger-Cats have captured a Grey Cup title in every decade of the 20th century — a feat matched by no other professional sports franchise except the Montreal Canadiens. Although they were named the Hamilton Tigers for their first 81 years, Hamilton's football club has been in existence for 139 years.

Although the franchise has had its ups and downs, this is a city that bleeds black and gold. Few Hamiltonians could not complete the Ticats' rather odd cheer that begins "Oskee-Wee-Wee."

The Tiger-Cats have had some phenomenal runs. From 1950 to 1972, the franchise came first in their division 13 times, appeared in the Grey Cup 11 times and won it six times. It made household names out of people like Angelo Moska and Garney Henley, and not just in Hamilton but across the country. In total the team has won the Grey Cup 15 times.

Hamilton teams have always been characterized by hard-fighting defences. Hard-hitting heroes are never more popular than on Labour Day, when the city plays the hated Toronto Argonauts that Hamiltonians view as an ideological contest of grit and grime versus that of glitz and glamour.

Community support hasn't always translated into financial health, particularly through tumultuous years following the 1989 sale of the team by Toronto Maple Leafs owner Harold Ballard. As recently as 2003, the Tiger-Cats went into receivership before being bailed out by current owner Bob Young. In 2004, the team drew more than 250,000 fans for the first time in their history.

Did you know...

that there is an African Lion Safari on the outskirts of the city? First opened in 1969, it has 1,000 animals of over 38 species. It has been successful breeding 30 species that are considered endangered and 20 or more species considered threatened.

Rudolf and Frieda Denninger opened their store on King Street East in 1954, six months after emigrating from Germany. The stores offer a huge selection for adventurous chefs, including Denninger's famous sausage and a variety of specialty soups. There is a huge range of British and European foods, including meats, sausages, desserts, sauces, cheeses, chocolate and breads, as well as various ingredients essential for Asian and other exotic dishes.

FAST FOOD

- Number of Tim Horton's in Canada: 2,733
- Number of Tim Horton's in Hamilton: 69
- Number of McDonald's in Canada: Over 1,400
- Number of McDonald's in Hamilton: 17
- Number of Subway's in Canada: 2,306
- Number of Subway's in Hamilton: 17

Did you know...

that the Hamilton Golf and Country Club, founded in 1894, has hosted the Canadian Open four times?

Did you know...

that the Tiger-Cats were the only Canadian team to have ever defeated a National Football League team? In 1961, they beat the Buffalo Bills by a score of 38–21.

SPORTS

When you think of sports and Hamilton you probably think football and the Tiger-Cats. But Hamilton is more than a one-sport town. The Hamilton Bull Dogs of the American Hockey League and a farm team of the Canadiens won the AHL championship, the Calder Cup, in 2007. Because of the geography of the city, the 2003 World Road Cycling Championship was held in Hamilton. This was one of the very few times this prestigious event was held outside of Europe and it brought tens of thousands of fans to the city while millions watched on TV all over the world.

Did you know...

When the first Around the Bay Marathon was held in Hamilton in 1894, the winner was Billy Marshall with a time of two hours and 14 minutes? The record to date is held by Joseph Ndiritu with a time of 1:32:53 in 2000.

Weblinks

City of Hamilton
http://www.myhamilton.ca/myhamilton
Follow the links to get details on museums and cultural events in the city.

Arts Council of Hamilton
http://www.artshamilton.ca/
Everything from literary and theatre listings to an arts calendar and gallery.

Hamilton Entertainment and Convention Facilities
http://www.hecfi.on.ca/
Your source for what's going on in Hamilton.

People

For about 6,000 years, humans have lived in the area around the western tip of Lake Ontario — known to the first European settlers as Head-of-the-Lake, and later as Hamilton. The first aboriginals to settle in the area called the Hamilton bay "Macassa," meaning "beautiful waters."

The area was once the centre of the territory of a group of natives known as the Attiwandaronks, who fished the shorelines, hunted in the forests and grew squash and corn. Believed to have numbered about 40,000 prior to the arrival of Europeans, the population of Attiwandaronks was decimated by a smallpox epidemic between 1638 and 1640.

The Hamilton-area natives were called the Neutrals by French explorers, because they remained neutral between the two dominant groups in the region: the Iroquois who lived south of Lake Ontario, and the Hurons who lived along Georgian Bay.

Although Mohawk Road and King Street were both part of native trails leading from settlements on the Grand River to the mouth of the Niagara River, the area of the city below the escarpment never developed any large-scale settlements due to its marshy nature.

By 1700, the area was established as French territory. Fur trading posts existed in Toronto and at the mouth of the Niagara River, while Dundas may have served as a storage depot for traders to store furs and trading goods. By that time, there was no evidence of the Attiwandaronks, and the territory was being occupied by the Mississaugas of the Ojibwa Nation.

In the 2006 census, only 1.5 percent of the Hamilton population — or 7,625 people — identified themselves as Aboriginal.

TOP TEN LANGUAGES SPOKEN IN HAMILTON

English	91.5 percent
Italian	3.3 percent
Polish	1.6 percent
French	1.5 percent
Portuguese	1.4 percent
Chinese	1.3 percent
Serbian	1.0 percent
Croatian	1.0 percent
Arabic	1.0 percent
Spanish	0.9 percent

Source: Statistics Canada.

ETHNIC ORIGIN OF HAMILTON'S POPULATION (PERCENTAGES)

	1871	1921	1971
Canada	52.8	61.2	69.8
United Kingdom	40.2	28.9	9.8
Europe	2.2	5.7	17.6
United States	4.6	3.4	1.0
Asia	—	0.4	0.8
Other	0.2	0.4	0.8

Source: Census of Canada, 1871-1971.

Bio REVEREND JOHN C. HOLLAND

More than 50 years after his death, John Holland's name lives on in Hamilton. Since 1996, the Hamilton Black History Committee has given an annual award in his name to recognize achievement and volunteerism in the city's African-Canadian community.

A former pastor of Stewart Memorial Church on John Street North, Reverend John Holland was born in 1882 in Hamilton to former slaves who escaped to Canada via the Underground Railway. Holland's father returned to the United States to fight with the Union Army during the American Civil War, then returned to Hamilton to operate a feed store on Mary Street.

While working as a porter with the Toronto, Hamilton & Buffalo (TH&B) Railway, Holland studied to become an ordained minister. In 1924, at the age of 42, he received his ordination and became an assistant minister, then later pastor of the John Street North church.

He is credited with helping to keep the church open through the financially difficult times of the Great Depression.

Over his career with TH&B, Holland worked his way up to become head Porter, then eventually a private car attendant, before retiring in 1948 to dedicate himself to full time work with the church.

In 1953, he was selected as Hamilton's Citizen of the Year — the first African-Canadian to earn that recognition. In 2003, he was inducted posthumously into Hamilton's Gallery of Distinction, in honour of his use of "faith, hope and determination to minister to those around him."

Today, Stewart Memorial Church is designated as an Ontario Heritage Site in recognition of its service to the longest surviving predominantly Black congregation in Hamilton. Its history affirms its importance as both a religious and a social centre for the city's community of African decent.

TOP 10 CURRENT PLACES OF BIRTH FOR IMMIGRANTS TO HAMILTON

Yugoslavia	7.7 percent
Poland	6.5 percent
India	6.4 percent
China	5.4 percent

Take 5 LARRY DI IANNI'S MEMORIES
OF ARRIVING IN CANADA

In 1956, a nine-year-old boy from the small Italian village of Villetta Barrea arrived in Hamilton to build a new life with his family. Forty-six years later, in 2003, Larry Di Ianni was elected to the position of mayor of his adopted city.

As part of the thriving Italian community that has helped shape Hamilton's landscape and culture, Di Ianni spent his career as a teacher and high school principal, while serving as a member of Stoney Creek council from 1982 until amalgamation in 2001. After one term as a councillor for the new city of Hamilton, he served as mayor from 2003 to 2006.

1. **Santa Claus:** As we landed in Halifax in early December, I was drawn to a store window featuring a small, mechanical Santa Claus welcoming port visitors and immigrants. We didn't celebrate Santa in Italy then, although I had heard about this magical elf. I interpreted these gestures as my personal salutation into the country.

2. **On Being Renters:** My family rented the second floor of a home on Stirton Avenue. Another family resided on the first floor. We were told NOT to make any noise lest the landlords would kick us out. What a disappointment. I wanted to run and shout with joy.

3. **On Being Owners:** We bought a home on Cannon Street, near Sherman Avenue. It was great to have our own home, except that boarders moved into the second floor. We were told NOT to make

Philippines	5.2 percent
Iraq	5.2 percent
Bosnia and Herzegovina	4.4 percent
Pakistan	4.0 percent
United Kingdom	3.9 percent
Croatia	3.7 percent

Source: Statistics Canada, Canadian Labour and Business Centre.

any noise lest the renters decided to move elsewhere. I found little difference between renting and owning.

4. **My First School Day:** My first day at St. Ann's School was bitter-sweet. I was happy to start school even though they put me in grade two, when age-wise I should have been in grade four. I suppose this was the 50's equivalent of ESL programming.

I wore my Sunday-best knicker pants to school, and I recall the first lesson vividly. The class was studying spelling. There was a picture of a baseball player on the page and he was also wearing knickers as part of his baseball uniform. Peter, the boy ahead of me, pointed to the picture and to my pants and asked with a hitting motion of his hand if I too were a baseball player. I had never seen baseball in my life, but I nodded, 'yes'. The desire to be accepted was strong.

5. **Renzo Teaches Romolo:** After several months of school, my English improved somewhat. When Ray, another Italian boy whose real name was Romolo (they re-baptized all of us in those days; my real name was Renzo and I became Larry on a teacher's insistence), came to class, the teacher asked me to translate for him. She rattled off instructions — only half of which I understood. I confidently trans-lated for Ray, making up what I hadn't quite grasped. Ray was none the wiser for it; and no great disasters of logistics seemed to occur. Sometimes one has to be born lucky, and Ray and I clearly had been!

UNITED EMPIRE LOYALISTS

Following the American Revolution, about 10,000 United Empire Loyalists came to settle in what is now southern Ontario. About 2,000 arrived in the Niagara Peninsula area, including Head-of-the-Lake.

Each Loyalist family could claim 200 acres of land to settle, purchased from First Nations people by Britain to provide for those who had supported it during the war.

Take 5 FIVE FAMOUS IRISH HAMILTONIANS

1. **Victor Copps.** Honoured as the 1989 Irish Person of the Year, Copps served as the city's mayor from 1962 until 1976. Hamilton's first Roman Catholic mayor, Copps was well-known for his work on the downtown urban renewal project that resulted, among other things, in the building of the hockey arena named Copps Coliseum.

2. **Martin Short.** Born in Hamilton in 1950, the famous comedian's father came to North America as a stowaway Roman Catholic refugee from Belfast, Northern Ireland. The actor, writer and producer was named a Member of the Order of Canada in 1994.

3. **Ron Joyce.** A former Hamilton police officer, Joyce co-founded the famous coffee and donut chain with hockey player Tim Horton.

4. **Kathleen Blake.** Born in Ireland in 1864, Blake was the best-known female journalist of her time. At the age of 25, she became the first full-time women's page editor in Canada. A highly acclaimed foreign affairs correspondent during the Spanish-American War, Blake also founded the Canadian Women's Press Club, which became the Media Club of Canada. McMaster University offers a yearly scholarship in her memory.

5. **Pat Quinn.** Former NHL player and coach, Quinn was born in Hamilton in 1943 and began playing hockey at an outdoor rink on Parkdale Avenue. A section of Glennie Street where he grew up has been renamed Pat Quinn Way, and the nearby arena has been renamed the Pat Quinn Parkdale Arena.

They Said It

"Irish and foreigners need not apply."
– **A sign posted on the gate of Hamilton's Procter & Gamble
plant during the Depression of the 1930s.**

In 1786, Richard Beasley was one of the earliest settlers to the area, eventually building a home on the Burlington Heights site now home to Dundurn Castle. Beasley's son Henry is recorded as the first child of European origin born at Head-of-the-Lake. By 1791, a total of 31 families were recorded as living at Head-of-the-Lake.

IRISH

The first Irishman to settle in Hamilton was William Gage, who in 1790 established a Stoney Creek farm that would be the site of the Battle of Stoney Creek during the War of 1812. Gage, however, was hardly typical of later Irish immigrants to the city.

The majority of those who came to Hamilton from the Emerald Isle were impoverished and landless, driven mainly by economic hardship in Ireland and Canadian demand for labour in the early 19th century. Between 1832 and 1848, Irish immigrants flooded the city in such numbers that they grew from 12 percent of the population to 30 percent.

In one week alone in June 1833, more than 300 Irish immigrants were added to Hamilton's small population of a little over 1,000 people. In 1847, following the Irish Potato Famine, over 3,000 people landed in the city in a five-month period.

Did you know...

that 17 percent of Hamilton's public school students have a first language other than English and that 72 languages are spoken in the school board?

They Said It

"Genealogy has become the one hobby that I am really passionate about. It probably has to do with the realization that I can find my roots even though my ancestors belonged to the lowest stratum of society, that they were among the poorest, that some of them were not much more than slaves or serfs ... that they were illiterate, but that somehow they persevered, survived against many odds. And that -- as a result -- here I am today and here are my two sons who will also remember their ancestors."

– Dr. Malgorzata Nowaczyk, a clinical geneticist with Hamilton Health Sciences, *Hamilton Spectator*, Dec. 28, 2005.

CANAL WORK

Thousands were employed digging and building the Burlington Bay, Desjardin and Welland Canals, and after that working on the railways. Men also worked in city construction and on the wharves, while unmarried women sought work as domestic servants to the town's elite.

Many of the Irish newcomers settled in the area at the foot of the escarpment east of John Street. The first map to identify the area as Corktown was published in 1842, although it isn't clear why it was given that nickname, as most of the early Irish settlers were from the Munster areas of Kerry, Limerick and Clare.

In the boggy, poorly-drained area, the newcomers built their homes on rented properties and developed a vibrant neighbourhood of Irish-style 'groceries.' The groceries saw front parlours of houses converted into combination shops and pubs that offered food and drink, and developed into neighbourhood hubs for gossip, music and conversation.

Did you know...

that Hamilton has the third highest proportion of immigrants in Canada behind Toronto and Vancouver at 24.4 percent?

Take 5 — ED DUNN'S FIVE BEST PLACES TO
CELEBRATE ST. PATRICK'S DAY IN HAMILTON

Ed Dunn, Hamilton's 2008 Irish Person of the Year, never misses a St. Patrick's Day celebration. Although he was born in Canada, his Irish roots go back to his great-grandfather, who lived in County Clare in Ireland.

1. The "Wearing of the Green" Irish Luncheon at Michelangelo's Banquet Centre is a wonderful way to celebrate St. Patrick's Day. Those who are Irish, along with those wanting to be Irish, celebrate over a lunch of corned beef, cabbage and potatoes. Over 350 people attended the 2008 celebration. Along with Irish dancers and musicians, the celebration features the honouring of an "Irish Person of the Year." The luncheon was established in 1986, with the first recipient being Bishop Joseph F. Ryan.

2. The Irish Monument at City Hall is a great place to celebrate our Irish background and thank our ancestors for their contribution to Hamilton. Get together with some Irish descendants and give thanks to those Irish settlers who have helped make the city a better place to live.

3. The Slainte Irish Pub, on Bowen Street, is usually full of people drinking, talking, laughing and singing to celebrate St. Patty's Day. I have enjoyed the times spent with friends and family members having some green beer and enjoying each other's company.

4. Ye Olde Squires Pub, on Fennell Ave East, is another great place to celebrate St. Patty's Day. We gathered there this year with family and friends to celebrate the honour of my being named "Irish Person of the Year" for 2008. We were also entertained by Irish musicians and dancers.

5. Celebrating with loved ones, no matter the location, is the best way to celebrate St. Patrick's Day. The joy of being able to celebrate with those whom I love gives me the warmest of feelings and a chance to be thankful to God for my many blessings.

THE CHURCH

Construction on St. Patrick's church began in 1876, following the purchase of a property east of Victoria Avenue by Irish Bishop P.F. Crinnon for $10,000. Irishman and architect Joseph Connolly built the church in the French Gothic style, with a bell tower and stained glass windows depicting various scenes, including one of Ireland and three of St. Patrick.

The 1830s saw the founding of the St. Patrick's Society of

Bio RAY LEWIS

Order of Canada appointee, Raymond Lewis was born in Hamilton in 1910 and passed away in 2003. He has the distinction of being the first Canadian-born Black athlete to stand at the victory podium and receive an Olympic medal in track and field. As the biography on the Governor General's website states, he trained "by running alongside the CP railway tracks and occasionally in farmer's fields." He was a member of the 4 by 400 meter relay team that won a bronze at the 1932 Olympics in Los Angeles. He also won a silver medal at the 1934 British Empire Games in London.

He attended Marquette University in Milwaukee but returned to Canada where he managed to find a job as a CP Rail porter. Hurdler Jim Worrall, Canada's flag bearer at the 1936 Olympics and a close friend, is quoted in the Sports Alliance online obituary saying that "Ray had some difficulties in his early years because of his colour. It's fair to say that he missed opportunities that he should have had. I recall in 1934 he was supposed to compete at the Canadian Olympic championships in Fort William but he couldn't get time off work — but then the CPR assigned him as porter on the train that took the team there. He didn't get to compete but he got to be with us."

Lewis worked as a porter until 1952 when he opened his own cleaning business in Hamilton — an endeavor that was not very successful.

Hamilton, a benevolent and cultural association formed to help incoming immigrants and organize social events. Although it has changed names and homes several times, the organization still exists today in the form of the Irish Canadian Club.

In addition to organizing annual St. Patrick's Day celebrations, the association has given birth to numerous bands and choirs, and for several decades, organized the Hamilton Feis.

Held annually on the July 1 weekend, the competition drew competitors and spectators from across Canada and nearby American states to take part in hurling and gaelic football games.

In 1958, he became chauffeur to a provincial cabinet minister. He then moved on to become a clerk at the Unified Family Court in Hamilton and worked at that until he was 78. He was also an active Mason and was honoured by them in 2001 for his service and for acting as a role model.

On July 1, 2000, Ray lit the torch for the opening of the International Children's Games held in Hamilton. The Ray Lewis Athlete Community Service Award was created and first presented in 2003. Lewis was a frequent speaker at schools around Hamilton and, the *Hamilton Spectator* reported, he would say about racism and discrimination that "some people say I'm bitter and should let it go but it happened and it was worse here because it wasn't supposed to happen. People shouldn't forget." He added that "things are clearly better for blacks and other minorities" but he lamented that racial discrimination continues. He believed the lessons of history are necessary so that incidents of racism diminish, not escalate and he is hopeful for the future.

In May 2005, Ray's widow, on her 92nd birthday, officiated at the opening of the Ray Lewis Elementary school in Hamilton by presenting a baton that her husband received from Queen Elizabeth in March 2002. The baton, a symbol of the Commonwealth Games, had contained a message to be read at the games in Manchester that year.

UNDERGROUND RAILROAD

Through the 1830s and 40s, African American slaves from the United States used the Underground Railroad to escape north to Canada. The first Black community in Hamilton settled along Concession Street, which was then called Stone Road, and established a community known as Little Africa.

By 1865, over 200 Blacks had established homes in the area bounded by Upper Wentworth, Upper Sherman, Concession and Fennell. The community was served by two churches, as well as 'the Mission' — a multi-purpose one-room building constructed in 1860, which was used as a school and religious building.

With no access roads yet constructed down the escarpment, finding work was difficult in the isolated community. Many worked on nearby farms, or for the railway industry, but by 1920 most of Little Africa's settlers had moved elsewhere.

In the 2006 census, 2.8 percent of Hamilton residents (13,900 people) identified themselves as Black.

Did you know...

that Hamilton's Irish-born sprinter Bobby Kerr, who won a gold medal at the 1908 Olympics, is a distant relation to Hamilton's longest running Mayor Bob Morrow?

Did you know...

that an 1851 census found that nine percent of Hamilton residents were born in Canada West (later Ontario), 29 percent were born in England or Wales, 18 percent came from Scotland, 32 percent emigrated from Ireland and eight percent were born in the United States?

They Said It

"The natural qualities of the sons of Italy — thrifty, of good morals, religious and fond of family life — make them excellent and desirable citizens..."

– The *Hamilton Herald*, May 1931.

NEW CULTURES ARRIVE

The 25 years prior to the World War I saw many new groups of immigrants arrive in Hamilton. Although there were still immigrants coming from Britain, Scotland and Ireland, many of the newcomers came to the city from eastern and southern European countries and brought new languages, religions and customs.

Evidence of a Jewish community in Hamilton can be found as early as 1853, with the establishment in the city of Anshe Shalom, a Hebrew Benevolent Society. However, the largest influx of Jewish newcomers came in the period prior to the World War I. The immigrants settled primarily in the northwest end of the city, in the neighbourhood around Queen and York Streets.

ITALIANS

In the 1890s, immigrants from Italy began coming to Hamilton to work as construction labourers on the Toronto, Hamilton and Buffalo (TH&B) Railway and in the area foundries and quarries. Most of the newcomers in the early years were young men seeking to earn money in North America, then return home.

Along with other foreign workers, they settled in the areas around Barton and Sherman Streets, often living in crowded boarding houses. In 1913, a *Report of a Preliminary and General Social Survey of Hamilton* outlined the dismal living conditions faced by many immigrant workers.

In a one-block area adjacent to Sherman Street, the report notes that 263 people were living in 18 houses. Of those, 232 were men, 19 were women and 12 were children. It also notes that 134 of the residents were Italian, 79 were Bulgarian, 29 were Polish, 12 were from Romania and 10 were Macedonian.

By 1912, the Italian community had established St. Anthony's church, and supported its own newspaper, *L'Italia di Hamilton.* By World War I, it was estimated that about 5,000 Italians were living in Hamilton.

In the mid-1920s, Hamilton's Italian community was instrumental in the formation of the Sons of Italy in Ontario, an important cultural and social group for the community.

THE SECOND WAVE

A second, larger wave of Italian immigrants came to the city following World War II. Leaving a war-impoverished country, most of the immigrants came from southern Italy seeking economic opportunities.

A booming economy in Canada offered good job prospects, and Hamilton's construction and steel industries welcomed the newcomers. By 1961, about six percent of the city's population or more than 17,500 residents claimed Italian heritage.

In 2001, Hamilton boasted the fourth largest number of Italian Canadian citizens (67,685), behind Toronto, Montreal and Vancouver.

Source: Italians in Ontario, Hamilton — An Illustrated History.

AFTER WORLD WAR II

In the 15 years following the end of World War II, more than 50,000 immigrants arrived in Hamilton. Some came to Canada as brides of returning servicemen, while others were fleeing Soviet-controlled areas of Europe. Many were seeking economic opportunities for them-

Did you know...

that both St. Peters and St. Joseph's Hospital were established by Irish-born clergymen?

selves and their families.

Newcomers from Lithuania, Latvia, Estonia, Poland, Serbia, Croatia, Hungary, Portugal and elsewhere helped shape the city's culture. While most eventually scattered throughout the city, pockets of ethnic neighbourhoods can still be found, particularly in the downtown core.

Today, Hamilton has the third highest percentage of foreign-born residents in Canada, behind only Toronto and Vancouver. The city welcomes more than 5,000 immigrants every year, with immigration accounting for about 85 percent of Hamilton's population growth.

Weblinks

Irish Hamilton

www.irishhamilton.ca

The webpage of Hamilton's Irish Canadian club, this site provides information about the city's Irish community, past and present.

Canadian Culture Online

www.culture.ca

This site offers a heritage section with cultural histories of many of Canada's immigrant groups.

Jewish Hamilton

www.jewishhamilton.org

Come here to find information about Hamilton's Jewish community, including local events and news.

Did you know...

that in 1954, Stelco boasted that over half of the nations in the world were represented among its 15,000 employees?

Then and Now

When the first settlers first came to present day Hamilton, they called it Head-of-the-Lake. They could not have imagined what lay ahead. The Head-of-the-Lake, as it turns out, was to become one of the most prosperous cities in one of the most prosperous areas in a new country called Canada.

The area's access to the Great Lakes transportation system, as well as its proximity to both Toronto and the American border, probably destined it to become an important centre. But much of the city's success can be laid at the feet of its people. From the early railroads, to the telephone and electric power, Hamiltonians have seized, built and improved upon technology. The story of Hamilton is a very human story.

POPULATION THEN AND NOW
1834 – 1,367
1845 – 6,478
1854 – 18,596
1867 – 21,485
1880 – 35,009
1890 – 44,653
1900 – 51,561

1920 – 108,143
1940 – 154,915
1960 – 258,576
1980 – 306,640
2001 – 490,268
2006 – 504,559

Sources: Hamilton Public Library Historical Archives, Statistics Canada.

AVERAGE NUMBER OF PEOPLE PER HOUSEHOLD

1834 – 8
1848 – 6
1871 – 5.6
1901 – 4.9
1921 – 3.9
1941 – 4.2
1961 – 3.7
1981 – 2.7
2001 – 2.6

Source: Hamilton: An Illustrated History, Statistics Canada.

GOING MOBILE

Hamilton saw its first "horseless carriage" in 1898, when textile manufacturer John Moodie imported a one-cylinder Winton from Cleveland. Moodie would later be one of the founders of the Hamilton Automobile Club in 1903. The city had all of 18 cars then.

In 1914, Canada's first concrete highway connected Hamilton to Toronto, and by 1919 the Ontario Department of Highways recorded 4,948 passenger vehicles in the city — one for every 21.8 residents.

Did you know...

that Hamilton has had 19 Royal visits? The first was in 1860 when Edward, Prince of Wales (later King Edward VII) visited the city. The most recent was in 2002, when Queen Elizabeth II came to Hamilton.

Take 5 ORIGINS OF FIVE
HAMILTON STREET NAMES

1. **Gage Avenue:** Named after Robert Russell Gage, the street runs along the western boundary of Gage Park. (Gage Park was created after the well-known local lawyer sold 46 acres of land to the city in 1918.) Gage was the great-grandson of the family who settled on land in the Stoney Creek area, some of which is now preserved as Battlefield Park.

2. **Brucedale Avenue:** Named for well-known mountain resident William Bruce. The street was called Brucedale to avoid conflict with a Bruce Street in the lower city. In 1860, Bruce purchased eight acres of property and built a house he called "The Elms" at 101 Brucedale Avenue East, as well as an observatory to indulge his hobby as an amateur astronomer. In 1936, his daughter donated the bulk of his property to the city to create Bruce Park.

3. **Case Street:** Running between Sherman Avenue and Lottridge Street, this street was named for Hamilton's first physician, Dr. William Case. From 1809 when Dr. Case first arrived in Hamilton until 1820 he was the only physician in the district.

4. **The Jolley Cut:** A main access road up the mountain, the Jolley Cut was named after James Jolley, a saddle and harness maker who had a successful business downtown and a home on Concession Street at what is now East 15th Street. In the 1860s, the only road up the mountain that was large enough to carry a carriage was a toll road. Jolley, who apparently hated tolls, obtained permission from the city to build a free road up the escarpment. Once completed in 1873, Jolley deeded the road and its maintenance to the city on the condition that it would never be tolled. In his honour, the road was named the Jolley Cut.

5. **Sanford Avenue:** Named after William Eli Sanford, co-founder of Sanford, McInnes & Company, a clothing manufacturing company located on the corner of King and John Streets. The company grew to be the largest clothing manufacturer in the country, and in the 1880s was Hamilton's largest employer, with more than 2,000 workers. Sanford, a good friend of Sir John A. Macdonald, was made a senator in 1887.

Source: Hamilton Street Names: An Illustrated Guide.

NUMBER OF REGISTERED PASSENGER VEHICLES IN HAMILTON

1919 – 4,948
1925 – 11,524
1930 – 20,562
1935 – 21,066
1940 – 25,902
1950 – 39,016
1960 – 69,633
1968 – 96,706
1990 – 210,485
2004 – 242,294

Sources: Hamilton, An Illustrated History, Ontario Ministry of Transportation.

PUBLIC TRANSPORTATION

1874: The first horse-drawn cars get pulled along three miles of track. The service starts with six cars, each capable of carrying 14 to 16 passengers. The first route runs from Stuart Street west to James Street then north to Gore Park.

1880: Hamilton Street Railway headquarters is at Bay and Stuart Streets, where 50 horses and 20 streetcars are housed.

1892: The first electric streetcar goes into operation. The first two electric routes are along King Street and James Street. Streetcars continue running on Hamilton streets until April 1951.

Did you know...

that in 1905, on route to a fire, Fire Chief Alexander Aitchison was killed when his buggy was in a collision at the corner of King and Hughson Streets and he was thrown against the base of the Sir John A. Macdonald statue? As a result of the accident, the statue was moved from the middle of the intersection, turned to face east and relocated in Gore Park.

1890s: Radial trains (electric trams riding on rails) are established in Hamilton to offer passage to other communities. By 1913, 75 miles of electrified tracks run on four lines radiating out from downtown. Passengers can travel to Dundas, to Beamsville through Stoney Creek, Winona and Grimsby, to Brantford through Ancaster, and along the Beach Strip to Oakville and Burlington. Radials operate until 1930.

1926: The first motor bus arrives on Hamilton streets.

Studebaker: Canada'a Own Car

In August 1948, the first Studebaker rolled off a Hamilton assembly line and was marketed to the country as "Canada's Own Car." For nearly the next 20 years, Hamilton built Studebakers for the whole country.

Although Studebaker had produced cars in the Windsor area prior to World War II, it geared up Canadian production with a modern automobile factory on the 20-acre site of a former anti-aircraft gun plant it purchased from the Canadian government in 1947.

The floor space of the plant itself was about 325,000 square feet and when constructed, was one of the most modern factories in Canada. While engines for the vehicles were produced in the United States, the Hamilton plant assembled the famous cars and the company's half-ton pickup trucks from 1950 to 1955.

The early years of the operation saw the plant produce about 8,000 cars a year, and in its final years nearly 20,000 annually. The Hamilton police department supported Studebaker with the purchase of Studebaker Commanders for their fleet.

Although the Hamilton plant remained in operation after the collapse of the American company in 1964, it produced its last automobile on March 17, 1966. At that time, Studebaker was the tenth largest employer in the city with more than 600 employees.

In 2007, the Hamilton police force restored a 1964 Studebaker into a classic police cruiser, which is displayed at local festivals and events.

1940: Hamilton has 72 passenger streetcars and 33 buses in operation.

2006: The city's transit inventory is worth $153 million and includes 204 buses, 2,100 bus stops and 500 bus shelters.

ALL THE LIVE LONG DAY

At 2 am on January 18, 1854, a crowd of excited Hamiltonians welcomed the city's first train as it pulled into the Stuart Street Station. The Great Western Railway was up and running, almost 20 years after Sir Allan MacNab and other prominent local citizens began attempts to run rails through Hamilton.

Completion of the Great Western provided Hamilton with a rail link to New York, Boston and other American cities on the eastern seaboard, as well as to Detroit, Chicago and the American Midwest. Branch lines linked the city to Toronto, as well as to outlying rural communities looking to transport products to Hamilton for shipping out of the harbour.

Rail transportation replaced the often slow passage of goods and materials on steam ships through the Great Lakes and St. Lawrence Seaway, and was essential to Hamilton's development as an important industrial centre.

In 1888, the Great Western amalgamated with the Grand Trunk Railway, and in December 1895, the Toronto, Hamilton & Buffalo (TH&B) began serving the city. The TH&B went out of business in 1897 and its station and lines were acquired by GO Transit.

Did you know...

that tolls were charged on the Skyway Bridge from its opening in 1958 until December 28, 1973? Although most Hamiltonians never refer to the bridge as anything but the Skyway Bridge, its official, but rather awkward name is the Burlington Bay James N. Allan Twin Skyway Bridge.

HOLD THE LINE

Credit the game of chess for giving Hamilton the right to brag about being the site of the first telephone exchange in the British Empire.

Hamilton banker and stockbroker Hugh Cossart Baker Jr. witnessed a demonstration of Alexander Graham Bell's invention at the

Take 5 NOTABLE DISASTERS
IN HAMILTON HISTORY

1. **Cholera epidemic of 1854:** Hamilton was the worst hit Canadian city when cholera killed 552 people in the summer of 1854. A large stone memorial in Section J of the Hamilton Cemetery commemorates the victims.

2. **Desjardins Canal Disaster:** A Great Western Railway passenger train was headed to Hamilton from Toronto on March 12, 1857, when a broken axle caused the train to crash off the Desjardins Canal bridge and plunge into the 18-inch thick ice on the canal below. The crash killed 59 and injured 18 of the approximately 100 people on board.

3. **Grand Trunk Railway accident:** On January 28, 1917, at the intersection of Ferguson Avenue and King Street, a Hamilton Street Railway car and a Grand Trunk Railway freight train collided. The train was derailed across King Street and eight people were injured.

4. **Spanish Influenza Outbreak of 1918-1919:** The highly-contagious and particularly lethal infection struck the city of Hamilton in October 1918. By January, hundreds were dead. 264 of the victims are buried in Hamilton Cemetery alone.

5. **Hurricane Hazel: On October 15, 1954**, Hurricane Hazel blasted Hamilton and the rest of Southern Ontario with 70 mile per hour winds and more than 11 inches of rain in 48 hours. The storm downed power lines and trees, flooded homes and caused landslides along the Mountain brow.

They Said It

"The city in 1803 was all forest. The shores of the bay were diffi-cult to reach or see because they were hidden by a thick, almost impenetrable mass of trees and undergrowth...Bears at pigs, so settlers warred on bears. Wolves gobbled sheep and geese, so they hunted and trapped wolves. They also held organized raids on rattlesnakes on the mountainside. There was plenty of game. Many a time have I seen a deer jump the fence into my back yard, and there were millions of pigeons which we clubbed as they flew low."

– John Ryckman, born in Barton, described the area in 1803 as he remembered it.

Philadelphia International Exposition in 1876. Within a year, he set up the first four-way telephone exchange in the downtown Hamilton area, stringing a telegraph line to the homes of his chess mates.

In 1878, Baker purchased the exclusive rights to telephone instal-lations in the counties of Hamilton, Wentworth and Haldimand and started his own telephone exchange with ten telephones. By 1880, Baker had 350 phones hooked up on his system and had installed a long distance line to Dundas. He had also received the charter for a national company called the Bell Telephone Company of Canada.

In December 1880, after putting Hamilton on the map of tele-phone history, Baker sold his interests in the company.

FIRE

In the city's early days buildings were largely made of wood, almost all of them with open fireplaces. Fire was an ever-present danger.

1847: City council establishes a volunteer fire department with two companies. The city owns two fire engines and an engine house.

1857: Hamilton Fire Department consists of eight companies with a total of 518 volunteer officers and men and total annual expenditures of $1,908.

Take 5 — TOM MINNES' FIVE
FAVOURITE DUNDURN ITEMS

Since 1987, Tom Minnes has worked at several museums in Hamilton, including Whitehern. He is presently the Collections Manager at Dundurn Castle.

1. A dining room chair with the MacNab family crest and motto. This chair was donated to Dundurn in 2006 by Margaret Pruden who had been a tour guide here for over 20 years. It came up for sale at a local auction house and is the only one we have of the original set of 24.

2. A ceremonial sword given to Sir Allan MacNab by the officers and men of the Gore Militia in recognition of his leadership in suppressing the Upper Canada Rebellion of 1837. This was one of a number of artifacts returned to Dundurn by descendants of Sir Allan during the centennial restoration completed in 1967.

3. The knighthood awarded to Allan MacNab by Queen Victoria in 1838 in reward for his leadership in the suppression of the Upper Canadia Rebellion. Another of the artifacts returned to Dundurn during the centennial restoration.

4. Sophia's Diary. Although only a copy of the original diary kept by MacNab's eldest daughter from his second marriage, this 1846 journal has helped illuminate the details of daily life at Dundurn during the time period.

5. Indoor plumbing. Installed in the home in 1848, the plumbing provided running water for baths and even flush toilets. It is an early example of such a luxury in the Hamilton area.

They Said It

"There are no rules on what buildings get to be monuments to our memories. Last year I got calls from people lamenting the passing of the Burger King that sat out in the parking lot of the Centre Mall and the Pizza Hut on the parking lot of a strip mall at Barton and Centennial. Those callers will be remembering good times there, the way seniors now talk of happy days at Renner's Soda Fountain downtown."

– Paul Wilson, Spectator columnist, June 10, 2006.

1879: A permanent paid force of nine members is created, with support from 24 men on call.

1888: 54 officers and men organize into six companies with total annual expenditures of $29,830.63.

1919: Hamilton is the first city in Canada to adopt a two-platoon system allowing day and night shifts. Previously, firefighters had to spend 24 hours a day at the station with only one day off each week. This change requires hiring an additional 38 men.

1934: 202 men are working out of 12 stations and a headquarters building. They have an annual budget of $400,000, 21 fire-fighting vehicles and a repair shop.

Did you know...

that a group of five Hamiltonians were the first to demonstrate that electric power could be transmitted over long distances? The men, known locally as the "Five Johns" because they all shared that first name, established the Cataract Power Company and built an electric generating plant at DeCew Falls near St. Catherines. In 1898, using the new idea of alternating current, they successfully transmitted power to Hamilton via transmission towers.

Did you know...

that in 1899, an incline railway carried passengers, wagons and horses up and down the Mountain at Wentworth Street? The price per ride was two cents for adults and one cent for children.

1972: 400 men and officers are employed in three platoons, each with an assistant deputy chief. There are four staff divisions; fire prevention, training, administration and operations, with an annual budget over $5 million.

2007: $84.7 million post-amalgamation budget, including emergency medical services (ambulance and paramedics).

Sources: Hamilton Public Library Historical Archives, City of Hamilton.

Take 5 FIVE HAMILTON FIRSTS

1. **1856:** The Daniel C. Gunn engine shop on Wellington Street North produces the first Canadian-built locomotives.

2. **1923:** The first radio in Canada is manufactured at Westinghouse in Hamilton.

3. **1925:** The first traffic lights in Canada go into operation at the Delta.

4. **1930:** The first British Empire Games (which are now called the Commonwealth Games) are held in Hamilton. The city constructs Civic Stadium (now Ivor Wynne Stadium) and the adjacent Jimmy Thompson swimming pool to host the games.

5. **1946:** Canada's first drive-in theater, The Skyway, opens in Stoney Creek.

They Said It

"We've never landed such a fish as this ... Our whole development has been on mechanics lines. And the result has been, the owners don't live here...and Hamilton has become too much of a factory town. This is the first break toward a broader culture and higher educational development."

– Thomas McQuesten, on why Hamilton "sorely needed" McMaster University.

EDUCATION

When Central Public School opened its doors to 600 students in 1853, it was the first graded public school in Canada. Replacing a number of one-room schoolhouses in the area, it adopted a model advocated by leading education reformers of the time. The reformers believed that children should be taught a standard curriculum by grade and by teachers specializing in various subjects.

The city was also in the forefront of educational progress in 1861, when a group of influential local Methodists established the Wesleyan Ladies' College, a residential school for young women located on what is now the site of the Royal Connaught Hotel. The school taught not only traditional 'women's subjects,' but also current science, literature and languages. It educated more than 2,000 women between 1861 and when it closed its doors 1890.

In 1931, when Westdale Secondary School was built, it became the largest composite school in the British Empire. The building came in at unheard of cost of $1.3 million. Today, the Hamilton-Wentworth District School Board serves 51,310 students at 96 elementary and 18 high schools across the region. It has an annual budget of $440 million.

Did you know...

that in the First World War Hamilton had the highest enlistment rate of any centre in the country, with 10,000 men volunteering to serve? The city lost 2,000 of those soldiers, and an estimated 7,000 returned home wounded.

Take 5 FIVE HAMILTON GHOSTS

McMaster graduate Ivan Reitman may have directed the film *Ghostbusters* but he failed to bring his crew to Hamilton to exorcise the city of many of its ghosts. There are so many of them that a local company offers tours of haunted Hamilton. Here are five of the purported ghosts.

1. The woman in black may be the most famous. She lives in the old custom house which is now the Workers Arts and Heritage Centre. The ghost is believed to be a woman who arrived on an immigrant ship and then died on arrival. Her remains were buried on the grounds and she is now seen (or her presence felt by a bone-numbing coldness and anxiety) in the basement near the vault. It is believed that she is waiting for her sailor lover to come get her.

2. The Battlefield House museum in Stoney Creek and the original site of the Gage family homestead is thought to be visited by Mary Gage. She rearranges objects in the museum. The surrounding grounds are also thought to be inhabited by the ghosts of soldiers killed in the battle during the War of 1812.

3. At the corner of John and Augusta in the downtown core is a mouldy-looking house believed to be the home of the headless coach. History has it that as the town clocks struck midnight, a coach drawn by nothing set out and proceeded down Hunter Street. No one ever found out where it went to but it was seen again the next night.

4. Colin, the bartender at the Glendale Golf and Country Club, passed away after 25 years service. Some nights, footsteps can be heard, along with the clinking of glasses.

5. A building, now used as the headquarters for the Hamilton and Region Conservation Authority, was once the site of the murder of 79-year-old John Heslop. His wife awakened him when she thought she heard burglars so he grabbed a lamp and went to investigate. Shots rang out and his wife found poor John dead on the landing. No one was ever caught for the crime and, to this day, his spirit can still be heard moving around at night.

They Said It

"It's the what-you-see-is-what-you-get, or wysiwyg, nature of the city and its citizens. In an age where everyone is trying to be hipper, cooler, or more popular than the next person, the genuine desire of Hamiltonians to be seen as exactly who they are is always an inspiration to an old typewriter salesman working in the trendy Internet business."

– Bob Young, Hamilton Ticat owner and Internet entrepreneur, on Hamilton's charm.

MCMASTER UNIVERSITY

Named after Senator William McMaster who left an endowment to create "a Christian school of learning," the small Baptist school was lured to the city from Toronto by prominent local lawyer and politician Thomas McQuesten.

As head of the Parks Board, McQuesten offered the university 50 acres of property, and committed to developing a park-like setting for the campus and establishing a citizen committee charged with raising $500,000 for the school. In 1930, McMaster University officially opened its doors to higher learning in Hamilton with degree programs in arts and theology.

In 1957, the university became a non-denominational private institution, although it maintained its historic Baptist connection through the creation of a theological school, McMaster Divinity College. Today, McMaster enrols 23,000 full-time students, and has received national and international recognition for its innovative teaching programs in various medical fields.

Did you know...

that the British military built a vault for armament storage when it commandeered the Dundurn castle property during the War of 1812? When Sir Allan MacNab built his famous castle home 20 years later, he incorporated the vault and an existing stone cottage into Dundurn.

MOHAWK COLLEGE

Officially born in 1967, Mohawk College has its roots in the founding of the Provincial Institute of Textiles in 1947, which offered technical training in textile manufacturing skills.

A decade later, the school evolved into the Hamilton Institute of Technology, offering courses in textiles, electrical, electronics and mechanical technology. In 1967, the institute was integrated into the newly-established Mohawk College. The first class of 220 Mohawk students studied out of a leased facility on Dundurn Street South while construction of the Fennell Avenue campus was underway.

Today, the college has an enrolment of 10,000 full-time post-secondary students, along with 3,000 apprenticeship students and offers a variety of academic, trade and technology programs.

HAMILTON'S MEDIA HISTORY

Far enough away from Toronto, and with its own identity and significant population base, Hamilton has always been well served by local media. At the turn of the 20th century, three separate newspapers were competing for Hamilton readers.

1827: *The Gore Gazette* and *Ancaster, Hamilton, Dundas and Flamborough Advertiser* begin publishing out of Ancaster.

1829: Hamilton's first newspaper, *The Gore Balance* is published. The paper folds the following year.

1833: Three weekly papers — the *Hamilton Free Press*, the *Western Mercury* and the *Canadian Wesleyan* begin publishing in the area.

Did you know...

that between 1971 and 2001, Hamilton lost 837 farms (a 45 percent decline) and saw 32,186 acres go out of production (a 19 percent decline)?

1835: The *Hamilton Gazette* newspaper launches; publication continues until 1856.

1846: The *Hamilton Spectator* newspaper begins publishing.

1858: The *Hamilton Times* newspaper launches and runs until 1920.

1889: The *Hamilton Herald* newspaper launches and is published until 1936.

1922: CKOC radio hits the airwaves.

1927: CHML radio begins to operate. Original station owners are the Maple Leaf Radio Company; the HML in the call sign stands for Hamilton Maple Leaf.

1954: CHCH television begins broadcasting in 1954 as a CBC affiliate.

1960: CHCH becomes Canada's first independent television station when it drops its CBC affiliation.

2008: Hamilton is served by one daily newspaper, numerous community and specialty publications, one television station, three AM radio stations, and six FM radio stations.

THE GREAT DEPRESSION

Although the Great Depression caused suffering across Canada, Hamilton was one of the hardest hit cities in Ontario because of its economic dependence on heavy industry.

Workers faced plant closures and layoffs. Companies that remained open operated with skeleton crews, and Stelco and Dofasco operated at only 40 to 50 percent capacity. By 1933, almost 25 percent of Hamilton families were on relief and the city was struggling to meet its welfare obligations.

The Great Depression did leave behind some positive legacies, however. The Rock Gardens at the Royal Botanical Gardens, along with the Sherman Cut were built by able-bodied men required to donate time to the city in exchange for relief payments.

The difficult times also inspired a group of Hamilton society's leading women to establish Canada's first birth control clinic. The Walnut Street clinic opened in 1932 and served 398 women in the first year despite its illegal status. Dr. Elizabeth Bagshaw, the clinic's first regular physician, offered her services to Hamilton women and families for 31 years, free of charge.

In 1937, following a court ruling legalizing birth control clinics, governments began providing funding for such services and Hamilton opened a second clinic on Kenilworth Avenue.

Weblinks

Hamilton Public Library

www.myhamilton.ca/myhamilton/LibraryServices/LocalHistory/
Provides links and listings of Hamilton Public Library material dealing with local history on a variety of subjects.

Head-of-the-Lake

www.headofthelake.ca
Web page of the Head-of-the-Lake historical society, which documents, preserves and promotes Hamilton history.

Studebaker Drivers Club

www.thehamiltonchaptersdc.ca
Website of the Hamilton chapter of the Studebaker Drivers Club. Contains photos and of what the earliest and last types of Studebakers produced in Hamilton looked like.

Politics

Although hardly more than a handful of people in 1816, the community of Hamilton was born when leading citizen and War of 1812 veteran George Hamilton convinced political friends to name the area as the judicial centre of the District of Gore.

The designation meant that citizens from across the district — made up of the counties of Wentworth, Halton, Brant, Haldimand and the Township of Puslinch — needed to travel to Hamilton to register property and deal with criminal charges or civil disputes. The decision also outraged citizens of the Town of Dundas who had asked for and were expecting to be given the right to establish a district courthouse and jail.

Fast-forward almost 200 years to the amalgamation of the city with Dundas, Ancaster, Glanbrook, Flamborough and Stoney Creek in 2001 and the competing interests of the outlying areas are still a dominant feature of Hamilton politics.

AMALGAMATION

The province-ordered amalgamation and the formation of the new city saw many of the suburbs dragged into a marriage against their wishes. While proponents argued that the merger would create efficiencies for the region, many residents in communities like Dundas and Flamborough feared higher taxes and a loss of community identity.

Amalgamation also resulted in the ousting of Hamilton's longest serving mayor — Bob Morrow — who lost his bid to head up the new city to Ancaster mayor Bob Wade, in a vote that pitted suburban residents against those living in the "old city of Hamilton."

Amalgamation has also resulted in somewhat schizophrenic representation at the provincial and federal government level. While the former city of Hamilton has long been known for electing colourful and left-leaning politicians such as former deputy Prime Minister Sheila Copps, the more affluent suburbs often send Conservative representatives to Ottawa and Queen's Park.

CITY GOVERNMENT TODAY

Officially incorporated as a city in 1846, Hamilton is now governed by a city council made up of a mayor and 15 councillors. The councillors each represent one ward, with eight councillors representing areas that were part of the former city of Hamilton and the remaining seven councillors representing amalgamated former suburban areas. The Mayor and Councillors serve four-year terms, with the next municipal election scheduled for November 8, 2010.

Although council is the final political decision-making body, much of the city's real work is done during meetings of its standing committees. Councillors participate in the following regularly-scheduled committees: Audit & Administration, Economic Development & Planning, Emergency & Community Services, Public Works, Board of Health and Committee of the Whole. A number of smaller committees, some with citizen representation, act in an advisory role to council.

Did you know...

that the federal riding of Hamilton West has been responsible for electing Canada's first female federal cabinet minister (Ellen Fairclough, 1957), its first black federal cabinet minister (Lincoln Alexander, 1979) and Canada's youngest MP (Sean O'Sullivan, age 20, 1972)?

They Said It

> "The imposition of amalgamation, over the most strenuous objections of taxpayers and their municipal councils, deprived residents of their inherent right to a democratic choice of local governance."
>
> **– Committee to Free Flamborough, in a July 2006 letter to Minister of Municipal Affairs John Gerretsen.**

OPERATING BUDGET

In 2007, the city's total expenditures topped $1 billion. City operations cost $900.2 million to run, and an additional $117.6 million was spent to run the Hamilton police department. The remaining $52.5 million was spent on assorted boards and agencies such as the public library, the Art Gallery of Hamilton and the local Conservation Authorities.

WHAT IT COST IN 2007

- Employment and Income Support: $147.5 million
- Fire and Emergency Services: $84.7 million
- Transit Services: $75.8 million
- Waste Management: $40.9 million
- Public Health Services: $35.7 million

WHERE THE DOLLARS COME FROM

- Local Taxpayers: $600 million
- Grants and Subsidies: $271.2 million
- Fees: $149.5 million
- Reserves/ Misc.: $37.5 million

CITY DEBT

- Outstanding Debt in 2007: $302 million
- Annual principal and interest payments on debt: $32.98 million

Did you know...

that in 1900, it was illegal to ride or drive a horse across King and James Streets faster than four miles per hour?

2007 TOTAL PROPERTY TAXES AND UTILITY CHARGES

Based on a 25-30 year-old detached three-bedroom, 1,200 sq. ft. bungalow on a 6,000 sq. ft. lot. Utility charges include telephone, power, water, sewer, land drainage and garbage collection.

Hamilton	$4,807
Toronto	$4,744
Ottawa	$4,680
Saskatoon	$4,671
Vancouver	$4,506
Regina	$4,397
Edmonton	$4,133
Halifax	$3,983
Calgary	$3,973
Fredericton	$3,957
Montreal	$3,815
Winnipeg	$3,529
St. John's	$3,328

Source: City of Edmonton, 2007 Residential Property Taxes and Utility Charges Survey.

VALUATIONS:

- Total assessed value of Hamilton properties 2007: $38.688 billion
- Total number of Hamilton properties 2007: 163,320
- Average property value 2007: $236,889
- Average value in 1998: $162,215
- Increase since 1998: 46 percent

Source: City of Hamilton, Region of Hamilton-Wentworth records.

Did you know...

that from 1847 until 1935, no Hamilton mayor served for more than two consecutive years? From 1936 until 2008, the city has had only 10 mayors — serving an average of 7.2 years each.

FEDERAL AND PROVINCIAL

Hamilton elects five of Canada's 308 Members of Parliament.

- In 2006, voters sent three members of the New Democratic Party (NDP) and two members of the Conservative Party to Ottawa.
- Hamilton elects five of Ontario's 107 provincial politicians.
- In 2007, the city elected two Liberals, two NDP members and one member of the Progressive Conservative party.
- The city currently has one provincial Cabinet Minister.

Bio THE HONOURABLE LINCOLN MACCAULEY ALEXANDER

Visitors to Hamilton might be excused for thinking that we just don't know how to spell very well. Why else would we call that highway The Linc, when it's so clearly a link?

But Hamilton residents know why the road is named after Lincoln Alexander. Not only did we name the time-saving stretch of road across the Mountain after him, in 2006 we voted him the Greatest Hamiltonian of All Time, in a contest organized by the *Hamilton Spectator*.

A McMaster graduate and Hamilton lawyer, Linc has had a lifetime of firsts. He was the first black Canadian elected to the House of Commons (1968), the first to be named a federal cabinet minister and the first to serve as Lieutenant Governor of any province.

In 2006, just months shy of his 85th birthday, he published his memoir, entitled, *Go to School, You're a Little Black Boy*. Linc explains the title as something his mother — a Jamaican immigrant who worked as a maid — often said to him while he was growing up.

"Those words, her words, have been at the core of what I've accomplished in my life," he says. "She was right, of course. My education has always been my empowerment."

Known for his support for youth and education issues throughout his political career, Linc now has several schools and a provincial youth leadership award named after him. His resume also includes serving as head of Ontario's Workers' Compensation Board, chancellor of the University of Guelph and chair of the Ontario Heritage Trust.

Hamilton Mayors through the Years

Name	Term	Profession
Colin Campbell Ferrie	1847	Banker
George Sylvester Tiffany	1848	Lawyer
William L. Distin	1849	Tinsmith
John Fisher	1850	Manufacturer
John Rose Holden	1851	Lawyer
Nehemiah Ford	1852	Painter
William G. Kerr	1853	Grocer
James Cummings	1854	Businessman
Charles Magill	1854-55	Storeowner
James Cummings	1856	Businessman
John Francis Moore	1857	Grocer
George Hamilton Mills	1858	Lawyer
Henry McKinstry	1859-61	Banker
Robert McElroy	1862-64	Contractor
Charles Magill	1865-66	Storeowner
Benjamin Ernest Charlton	1867	Teacher
Hutchison Clark	1868	Architect
James Edwin O'Reilly	1869	Lawyer
George Murison	1870	Builder
Daniel Black Chisholm	1871-72	Lawyer
Benjamin Ernest Charlton	1873-74	Teacher
George Roach	1875-76	Hotelier
Francis Edwin Kilvert	1877-78	Lawyer
James Edwin O'Reilly	1879-81	Lawyer
Charles Magill	1882-83	Storeowner
John James Mason	1884-85	Accountant
Alexander McKay	1886-87	Grain merchant
William Doran	1888-89	Grocer
David McLellan	1890-91	Insurance agent
Peter Campbell Blaicher	1892-93	Drugstore owner

Name	Term	Profession
Alexander David Stewart	1894-95	Chief of police
George Elias Tuckett	1896	Tobacco manufacturer
Edward Alexander Colquhoun	1897-98	Banker
James Vernall Teetzel	1899-1900	Judge
John Strathearne Hendrie	1901-02	Civil engineer
Wellington Jeffers Morden	1903-04	Real estate broker
Sanford Dennis Biggar	1905-06	Lawyer
Thomas Joseph Stewart	1907-08	Businessman
John Inglis McLaren	1909-10	Grocer
George Harmon Lees	1911-12	Jeweler
John Allan	1913-14	Builder
Chester Samuel Walters	1915-16	Accountant
Charles Goodenough Booker	1917-20	Tailor
George Charles Coppley	1921-22	Clothier
Thomas William Jutten	1923-25	Boat builder
Freeman Ferrier Treleaven	1926-27	Lawyer
William Burton	1928-29	Coal company owner
John Peebles	1930-33	Jeweler
Herbert Earl Wilton	1934-35	Journalist
William Robert Morrison	1936-43	Lawyer
Samuel Lawrence	1944-49	Stone mason
Lloyd Douglas Jackson	1950-62	Chemist
Victor Kennedy Copps	1963-76	Journalist
John Alexander MacDonald	1977-80	Plumbing business
William Powell	1981-82	Stelco employee
Robert Maxwell Morrow	1983-2000	Politician
Robert Wade	2001-2003	Insurance broker
Larry Dilanni	2004-2006	High school principal
Fred Eisenberger	current	Politician

RECENT POLITICAL SCANDALS BY THE NUMBERS

- $22,600: The amount of money Mayor Larry Di Ianni returned in illegal campaign contributions prior to pleading guilty to six charges of violating the Municipal Elections Act of Ontario in 2006.

- $500,000: The amount Liberal MP Tony Valeri was paid in 2005 for a Stoney Creek property he'd purchased three months earlier for $225,000. The sale was made to the son of Joe Ng, whose Hamilton-based company was a frequent contributor to the Liberals.

Facts About Hamilton Mayors

- Bob Morrow was Hamilton's longest serving mayor, holding the office from 1983 to 2000. First elected to City Council at the age of 24, Morrow was defeated in his bid to be mayor of the newly-amalgamated city by Bob Wade, who had served 16 years as the mayor of Ancaster.

- Hamilton's first mayor, Colin Ferrie, was one of the founders of the Gore Bank (1835), the London & Gore Railway (1834) and the Hamilton Board of Trade. He also served on the first Board of Police for Hamilton in 1833-34 and was elected to represent Hamilton in the House of Assembly in 1836.

- Chester Walters, elected mayor in 1915 at the age of 36, was a public accountant who went on to establish the Certified Public Accountants Association. After city politics, Walters went on to take charge of the province's finances. In 1935, he became Deputy Minister of the Ontario Treasury and comptroller of finances, a post he held for 18 years.

- Hamilton has never elected a woman to the job of mayor, although Nora Frances Henderson served as acting Mayor in 1946, when Mayor Sam Lawrence was out of the city.

Take 5 FIVE HAMILTON WOMEN
WHO LED THE WAY

1. **Alice Freel:** first woman to be part of the Saltfleet Township council (1926).

2. **Nora Francis Henderson:** first woman elected to Hamilton city council (1931), first woman to serve as Acting Mayor (1946).

3. **Ellen Fairclough:** first woman named a federal cabinet minister (1957), first mother elected to Hamilton city council.

4. **Anne Jones:** first chairman of the Regional Municipality of Hamilton-Wentworth (1973).

5. **Sheila Copps:** first female Deputy Prime Minister (1993).

- 24: The number of years Henry Merling held Hamilton's Ward 7 council seat prior to the 1997 municipal election. The week prior to the election, the *Hamilton Spectator* published stories showing that he was using his public office to operate a houseboat rental company whose customers included people who went to him for help at City Hall.

Did you know...

that in 1924, Hamilton became the first city in Ontario to pass a bylaw requiring stop signs on major thoroughfares?

Did you know...

that Ward 2, which covers the downtown area, is Hamilton's densest ward, with more than 16 eligible voters per acre? Ward 14, which covers rural Flamborough, is the city's least dense ward with only .114 voters per acre.

Take 5 FIVE HIGH POINTS
IN BOB WADE'S TERM AS MAYOR

As the first mayor of the "new" city of Hamilton, Bob Wade faced the difficult task of unifying Hamilton and the five suburban municipalities brought together in a forced marriage.

1. **Establishing the Strengthening Hamilton's Community Initiative (SHCI):** When arsonists torched Hamilton's Hindu Samaj temple in the days following the September 11 terrorist attacks, the city responded by bringing together a group of community leaders dedicated to building a community that values its racial, religious and cultural diversity. Fundraising efforts by temple members eventually generated over $1 million to rebuild and reopen the Hindu temple.

2. **Welcoming Queen Elizabeth II** in October 2002 as she visited Hamilton to present "new colours" to the city's Argyle & Sutherland Highlanders. I watched the ceremony with my wife Ida, and 18,500 spectators crowded into Copps Coliseum.

3. **Dedicating the Dieppe Veterans' Memorial Park:** During the 1942 raid on the French port of Dieppe, 582 soldiers from the Royal Hamilton Light Infantry (Wentworth Regiment) landed on French soil. During the eight-hour battle, 197 RHLI soldiers were killed and 174 were taken prisoner. More than half of the 211 soldiers who returned to England were wounded. To commemorate the 61st anniversary in 2003, the city dedicated the lakeside memorial park to those veterans.

4. **Hosting the Canadian Open:** In September 2003, the Hamilton Golf & Country Club welcomed 156 professional golfers to the country's most prestigious tournament, held in Hamilton for the first time since 1930.

5. **Hosting the World Cycling Championships:** A month after successfully welcoming the world's best golfers, Hamilton offered the world's best cyclists a venue to show off their skills. About 1,200 riders from 57 countries participated, while over 900 accredited members of the world media covered the event and broadcast to half a billion people around the globe.

Take 5 CLOSEST POLITICAL RACES
SINCE AMALGAMATION

1. **452 votes:** Fred Eisenberger over Larry Di Ianni in the 2006 race for mayor (54,110 to 53,658)
2. **304 votes:** Larry Di Ianni over Maria Pearson in the 2000 race for the Ward 10 (Stoney Creek) council seat (3,426 to 3,122)
3. **263 votes:** Russ Powers over Julia Kollek in the 2006 battle for the Ward 13 (Dundas) seat (2,667 to 2,404)
4. **123 votes:** Brad Clark over Phil Bruckler in the 2006 battle for the Ward 9 (Stoney Creek) council seat (3,394 to 3,271)
5. **85 votes:** Dave Braden over Don Robertson in the 2003 race for Ward 14 (Flamborough) councillor (2,350 to 2,265)

PLAYING CATCH

Hamiltonians are CATCH-ing up with news at City Hall. Since January 2004, a small group of dedicated volunteers has made it their mission to help keep residents informed about the detailed day-to-day decisions of municipal politicians.

CATCH — Citizens at City Hall — monitors, records and transcribes city council and committee meetings, and makes the transcripts available through their website.

"Municipal government is always described as the government closest to the people, but it's also the one that has the most impact on

They Said It

"Hamilton has been referred to as the 'Volunteer Capital of Canada' as more than 130,000 of our citizens volunteer each year. I never cease to be impressed with people who willingly give of their free time to ensure the success of whatever event is taking place. It has been said that unlike elections which are held every few years, volunteerism allows us to vote every day for the kind of community we make. It is the ultimate expression of democracy."
– **Bob Wade, Mayor of Hamilton (2001-2003).**

"Every provincial government makes decisions based not only on good public policy but also on partisan politics. It happens all the time. We see it all the time. They just don't acknowledge it, that's all."

– Ward 9 councillor Brad Clark, who served as a Progressive Conservative MPP from 1999 to 2003.

our day-to-day lives," says Don McLean, one of the founders of the organization. "We saw a need for more information to be part of the public debate and available to the public."

The group also writes news items that provide detailed information about city staff reports and city council discussions, including direct quotations taken from the meeting transcripts.

Along with posting them to the web site, CATCH e-mails several news bulletins a week to about 800 subscribers. The group sees its role as that of a neutral observer, explains McLean. It doesn't get involved in the political process except in cases where it is concerned with issues of public process or citizen access.

"We follow what the media does and try to avoid any duplication. We don't do detailed coverage of things that are being well covered in the media," says McLean. Without the space and time limitations of the traditional media, CATCH can provide a considerable amount of detail about issues, along with word-for-word reporting that gives citizens more information on issues and the position taken by their own ward councillor.

"I find doing this really rewarding because I think addition of information changes the discussion, enhances the process generally and has much more impact than ranting in an opinion piece," says McLean.

Did you know...

that the first form of public transit was established in 1874, when horse-drawn cars ran a route along James Street, then east along King Street to Wellington?

Bio SIR ALLAN NAPIER MACNAB

Little can be written about Hamilton's past without including the name of Allan Napier MacNab. Although he was best known as the builder of Dundurn Castle and as Premier of the United Canadas from 1854-56, MacNab was extensively involved in the most significant Hamilton events of his day.

MacNab was born in Niagara in 1798 to a Scottish military family (MacNab's father came to Canada as an aide to Lieutenant-Governor John Graves Simcoe). As a 14-year-old, the young MacNab fought in the War of 1812. He moved to Hamilton in 1826, where he set up a bustling legal practice. Within a few short years, he had made his fortune not from the law but rather in land deals. He very quickly became an important businessman in the district, serving on the boards of many important companies.

A staunch Tory, MacNab marshalled the forces of those in the area who supported the Family Compact against the Reform forces advocating responsible government. His big political break came in 1829 when he refused to testify before a committee of the House of Assembly that was investigating the hanging in effigy of Lieutenant Governor Sir John Colborne in Hamilton by a Tory mob. MacNab was sentenced to ten days in jail for contempt but in the process became a Tory martyr. In 1830, he was elected to the legislature of Upper Canada, a seat he would retain for 30 years.

In 1832, MacNab purchased the property known as Burlington Heights and spent the next three years building Dundurn. Built to impress, the house contained a formal dining room, separate family apartments (a total of 72 rooms), and introduced the young city to a new technological advance called indoor plumbing.

MacNab was involved in completion of the Desjardins Canal and the establishment of the first local bank, and was a major promoter of the Great Western Railway. He received a knighthood from Queen Victoria for his efforts in putting down the Upper Canada Rebellion of 1837. MacNab died at Dundurn on August 8, 1862.

DROWNING IN DEBT

Not unlike today's local politicians, those who governed Hamilton in the mid-19th century found there were always more projects to undertake than money to undertake them with.

The biggest of the municipal projects of the day involved the purchase of 50,000 pounds worth of stock in the Great Western Railway, and the construction of the city's waterworks. But by the 1850s, it became apparent that the city had overspent, with about 75 percent of expenditures going to pay interest on Hamilton's accumulated debt.

When the level of debt became known, and the taxation required to manage it became apparent, citizens began flooding out of the city. Hamilton's population dropped from more than 25,000 people in 1858, to 19,000 by 1862.

With creditors seeking and receiving judgements against the municipality, the city was ordered to place a special assessment on property taxpayers that would likely have encouraged additional people to flee Hamilton.

They Said It

"I've already said personally and very directly that if the GST is not abolished, I'll resign. I don't know how much clearer you can get. I think you've go to be accountable on the things that you say you're going to do and you have to deliver."

**– Hamilton East Liberal MP Sheila Copps,
October 18, 1993 on a CBC Town Hall program.**

They Said It

"I think that making a fast-lipped comment in an election campaign should not put me in a position to resign."

– Copps, April 26, 1996, CBC National, in response to the decision by the Liberals not to abolish the GST. Copps did eventually resign her seat in May 1996 but was re-elected in a June by-election.

However, city clerk Thomas Beasley decided it would be a good time for an extended holiday, and before he left, took the city's assessment rolls and locked them in a warehouse. His vacation lasted until the court term for the special assessment had expired. Beasley's move is seen to have saved the city from bankruptcy.

Despite that, Hamilton continued to struggle with its debt for years to come. In 1864, the city was still spending 86 percent of its tax revenues to service the debt, while in 1873, the debt ate up 50 percent of tax revenues.

Weblinks

City of Hamilton

www.myhamilton.ca

Provides access to city and library information, as well as links to many other community organizations and resources.

Citizens at City Hall (CATCH)

www.hamiltoncatch.org

Read detailed reports of the activities of city council and its various committees, written by volunteer citizen spectators.

Raise the Hammer

www.raisethehammer.org

A twice-monthly web magazine dedicated to Hamilton political issues, particularly in the area of urban development.

Crime and Punishment

CRIMELINE

1801: Mary Osborn London of Saltfleet Township becomes the first woman executed for murder in Upper Canada after she and her lover kill Mary's elderly husband.

1814: Concerned about pro-American sentiment during the War of 1812, authorities stage a show trial at Ancaster. Fifteen men are convicted of high treason and eight are executed at Burlington Heights, near the present-day site of Dundurn Castle.

1817: A two-storey log cabin on John Street is used as Hamilton's first courthouse.

1827: Hamilton's second courthouse is constructed on Main Street.

1828: George Young is banished from Ontario for seven years after being convicted of larceny in Hamilton.

1847: Hamilton's police force is established with four members.

1859: Three thousand people attend the hanging of John Mitchell. Convicted of murdering his common-law wife, Eliza Welch, Mitchell was the last person publicly hanged in Hamilton.

1877: Barton Street Jail opens.

1879: Hamilton's third courthouse opens.

Rocco

When Rocco Perri arrived in Canada in 1903, no one could have predicted he would become one of the wealthiest bootleggers of the Roaring '20s — and Hamilton's most famous missing person. Perri was among the thousands of Italian immigrants who worked in quarries and on construction sites, physically demanding jobs with little chance for advancement. Then, at 22, he fell in love with his 29-year-old landlady, Bessy Starkman, a married woman with two little girls. Bessie abandoned her family and moved with Rocco to St. Catharines.

At first times were tough. Rocco barely earned enough to buy clothing. But by 1915, the couple was running a grocery store on Hess Street North in Hamilton.

In 1916, Prohibition went into effect, bringing Rocco and Bessie a tremendous financial opportunity. They started selling bootleg booze for 50 cents a shot at the grocery store, gradually parlaying the profits into a fortune. In 1920, they bought a 19-room Victorian mansion at 166 Bay Street. They spent their money freely, but also gave generously to charities.

Flamboyant, wisecracking Rocco and Bessie, a petite soft-spoken blond, were devoted to each other and openly affectionate. But their

1885: Hamiltonians campaign to commute the death sentence of Maria McCabe, a teenage hotel servant convicted of infanticide. Her lover, a Hamilton businessman, refused to marry her after she became pregnant. Instead of going to the gallows, Maria serves less than seven years in Kingston.

1907: Accused of selling newspapers on a Sunday under the new Lord's Day Act, Hamilton vendor Louis Birk argues that since he stamped his papers "to be returned Tuesday" he was leasing, not selling, them. Unconvinced, the court fines him $30.

involvement in gambling, loan sharking, bank robbery, narcotics, and, reputedly, murder, inevitably made enemies among rival outlaws. On August 31, 1930, as the pair returned from an evening out, Bessie was gunned down in their garage. Her funeral was one of the most extravagant in Hamilton's history, with mourners and spectators lining the route to the Jewish cemetery on Highway 6.

Rocco survived two more attempts on his life. On one occasion, he was sitting in his car, talking to friends. When he turned the key in the ignition, the car exploded. Perri was thrown clear, but his friends were badly injured. On another occasion, someone tossed two sticks of dynamite under his front porch, and then detonated them. Perri was away from home at the time.

On April 23, 1943, Rocco Perri was staying with relatives in Hamilton. He complained of a headache, took a couple of painkillers, and then announced he was going for a stroll. He was never seen again. Police suspected foul play and reported they had good information that Perri was "in a barrel of cement at the bottom of Hamilton bay."

Officially the case remains unsolved; the fate of the man described as Hamilton's Al Capone remains a mystery.

Take 5   RECENT UNSOLVED MURDERS

1. **1998:** William Staples and his daughter Rhonda Borelli went missing in January 1998. In June, their bodies were found in the locked and covered box of Staples' 1997 white GMC Sonoma pick-up. The truck had been abandoned in the Park 'n Fly lot on Dixon Road, Toronto, not far from the airport. A $10,000 reward is offered for information leading to the arrest and conviction of the person or persons responsible for the murders.

2. **1998:** Criminal lawyer Lynn Gilbank and her husband Fred were killed in their bed in the early hours of November 16, 1998. Evidence suggests a number of people were involved in the murders, which are possibly linked to organized crime. Rewards for information leading to convictions have been offered. In addition, the police are offering immunity to those who played a minor role in the murders.

3. **2003:** John Daly, 34, was walking home when he encountered two men examining the inside of cars with flashlights. A neighbour watched him follow the two men north on East 34th street and then called the police. When police arrived a few minutes later, Daly was found a short distance away, unconscious and bleeding. He died ten days later in the hospital. Hamilton Police Services Board has approved a $10,000 reward for information leading to a conviction.

4. **2004:** Thelma Clapham, 79, lived alone in a Rebecca Street apartment. She was found bludgeoned to death on the morning of December 2. There was no sign of forced entry, and the police suspect that a woman was involved in the crime.

5. **2005:** Michael Palmer, 22, of Niagara Falls, New York, was shot at the corner of Roxborough Avenue and Ottawa Street North on September 9, 2005. He died of his injuries a few hours later. More than 100 people have been questioned and security videotapes examined, leading police to believe that the identity of Palmer's killers are known. The suspects include two black males in their early 20s and a white female. A reward of $10,000 is offered.

1919: Convicted murderer Paul Kowalski kills a guard and seriously injures two others in an unsuccessful bid to escape from the Barton Street Jail. Guard Arthur Awty becomes the only Hamilton jail guard ever killed on duty.

1929: Unable to pay a $200 fine for illegal possession of liquor, Ann Minnigan was sent to the Barton Street jail. Authorities were unaware that she was pregnant. She gave birth to premature twins, one of whom died. Outraged Hamiltonians, including the Local Council of Women, called for the appointment of a full time police matron. The Ontario government cancelled the rest of Minnigan's sentence.

1930: Bessie Starkman, bootlegger Rocco Perri's common-law wife and partner in crime, is gunned down outside their Bay Street home. The murder is never solved.

1943: Complaining of a headache, Hamilton underworld boss Rocco Perri takes two aspirins, steps outside for some fresh air, and vanishes.

1946: The headless torso of John Dick, a Hamilton Street Railway conductor, is found on the escarpment. Evidence points to his wife Evelyn, her father and her lover, and leads to one of the most sensational trials in Hamilton history.

Did you know...

that following the 1885 rebellion, former Hamilton police chief Alexander D. Stewart was chosen by the Canadian government to swear out a formal complaint against Louis Riel? He presented information to a stipendiary magistrate in Regina on July 6, 1886.

1953: Former church warden Harry Lee is the last man executed in Hamilton. Lee killed Mary Rosenblatt, a mother of two, and then shot himself. Although he concocted a story about being abducted, investigators determined he had killed Rosenblatt and then attempted suicide.

1956: Sixty teenagers mob two policemen, kicking and punching them as they try to break up a crowd at the Red Barn Restaurant on Beach Road.

Bio EVELYN DICK

On Saturday, March 16, 1946, children playing on the Hamilton escarpment found what they thought was the headless body of a pig. It turned out to be the torso of John Dick, a driver for the Hamilton Street Railway.

Investigation led to John's wife, the former Evelyn MacLean, an attractive young woman with a spotty history of illicit relationships and illegitimate children. Although Evelyn initially told a story of an Italian hitman who had been asking about her husband, bloodstains and a bullet hole were found in the basement of Evelyn's father's home at 214 Rossyln Avenue.

Detectives also discovered the body of an infant, encased in concrete, in the trunk in the attic of the Carrick Avenue house Evelyn had shared with John Dick. Under questioning, Evelyn implicated her lover, Bill Bohozuk, and eventually she, her father and Bohozuk were charged with murder.

The sensational trial riveted the attention of Hamiltonians. Could charming, delicate Evelyn, who baked cookies for courthouse staff during her trial, really have been involved in such a horrific crime?

The jury thought so. Evelyn was found guilty and sentenced to death. Her father, convicted of being an accessory to murder, was

1956: Two men attempt to rob the Royal Bank in Stoney Creek — one of them armed with a sickle. Alerted by the bank manager's cries, Police Chief Leonard Hockley runs from the police station across the street, revolver drawn, but hesitates to fire because the thieves have no guns. The thieves escape.

1958: Official opening of the five-story Hamilton courthouse, which is still in use today.

sentenced to five years in prison. Because Evelyn refused to testify against Bill Bohozuk, the case against him fell apart.

Evelyn's conviction was overturned on a technicality, but she was found guilty in the death of her infant son and sentenced to life imprisonment. She was paroled in 1958.

And then the real mystery surrounding Evelyn Dick began. There were rumors that she started a business, then married a wealthy man and lived in luxury. She certainly must have had powerful friends, as no one has successfully located her since her release. Still, reports of Evelyn Dick sightings circulated for years. Almost everyone in Hamilton either had a story about Evelyn or her family or claimed to really know what had happened to her. She inspired books, a stage play and a television movie.

In 1985, when Evelyn turned 65, she was granted a pardon. Her file was sealed and she no longer needed to report to the parole board. Although in 1987 there were rumours that a woman accidentally killed by stove fumes in Binbrook, south of Hamilton, was really Evelyn Dick, the story was never proven.

Evelyn Dick, now in her late 80s, remains as fascinating elusive as she has been since 1958.

They Said It

"Each of you are to be taken from the place from whence you came and from thence you are to be drawn on hurdles to the place of execution, whence you are to be hanged by the neck, but not until you are dead, for you must be cut down while alive and your entrails taken out and burned before your faces, your head then to be cut off and your bodies divided into four quarters and your heads and quarters to be at the King's disposal. And may God have mercy on your souls."

– The punishment planned for the Ancaster treason trial in 1813. The Ancaster trial became known as the Bloody Assize and is commemorated today with a historic plaque on Wilson Street East in Ancaster.

1958: Vending machine operator Donald Stewart rigs a flash camera in a coffee vending machine to foil robbers at the Robinson Cone Company plant on MacNab Street. The camera snaps a photo when the vending machine door is opened. The resulting photograph leads to the arrest of two men.

1960: German Shepherds King and Sandy become the first dogs used on the Hamilton police force.

Did you know...

that during the frequently violent Hamilton Street Railway Strike in 1906, police were called out to keep the peace? On November 23, in an effort to protect strikebreakers from a mob, they fired over the heads of the crowd. In the ensuing fracas they lost several of their new Colt revolvers.

1961: Police recover $5,000 in silverware, cash, radios and other objects from the Desjardins Canal after receiving a tip on the location of loot from a string of robberies.

Church of the Universe

Founded in Hamilton in 1969, the Church of the Universe has become one of Canada's most vocal advocates for the legalization of marijuana. Walter Tucker established the church in 1969, and for many years its large rural property between Hamilton and Guelph was a haven for those who wished to practice nudism, alternative spirituality and smoke marijuana in peace. Adherents call marijuana the Tree of Life and regard smoking it as a sacrament.

In the early years of its existence, members of the Church of the Universe were generally tolerated by law enforcement authorities. But in 1975, a body was found on the property and investigation uncovered connections with biker gangs. Police started keeping a closer eye on the group and a number of charges were filed. In 1994, one of its ministers, Brother Daniel Morgan was murdered in his own home. At the time, he was running for Hamilton council.

By this time, the Church of the Universe was deeply involved in a legal battle, claiming that the Controlled Drugs and Substances Act was unconstitutional. At the forefront of the battle were Brother Walter Tucker, the founder, and his close friend Brother Michael Baldasaro, who once ran for the position of Hamilton mayor.

In November 2007, Baldasaro and Tucker were convicted of drug trafficking. In late April 2008, they were sentenced to jail terms. Baldasaro, 58, was given two years in a federal prison for two counts of trafficking. Tucker, 75, received a 12-month jail sentence.

Handing down the sentence, Superior Court Justice John Cavarzan stated, "554 Barton Street East is a marijuana convenience store that operates for profit like a prohibition-era speakeasy, but disguised as a church."

> "You cut off his legs...
> You cut off his arms...
> You cut off his head...
> How could you Mrs. Dick?
> How could you Mrs. Dick?"
>
> **– Popular schoolyard song of the 1940s.**

1969: Block Parents starts in Hamilton.

1974: The "Phantom Flyer," who claims to be the ghost of World War I air ace Billy Bishop, steals a Piper Cherokee from Peninsula Air Services at Hamilton Civic Airport, Mount Hope, and sets it down at Peter's Corners, once on May 27, and again on June 17. He also "borrows" planes from King City Airport, north of Toronto, and Brampton Airport.

1974: After robbing a "body-rub parlor," a 22-year-old armed robber dubbed "The Kissing Bandit" apologizes to the 19-year-old female employee after receiving more than $200 in cash, then kisses her on the cheek. Unimpressed, she picks his face out of police mug shots.

1977: Police and the Crown Attorney's office express concern about a how-to book, *Crime Pays*, after a 17-year-old Dundas teenager follows it to plan a bank robbery. The crime went awry when the teller threw the would-be bandit's note back at him and ran to inform a colleague. The teenager was placed on three years probation.

Did you know...

that the Downtown Centre (also known as the Old Courthouse) is said to be haunted? People have reported hearing footsteps or catching a fleeting glimpse of someone on the fourth floor of the building.

1997: Johnny "Pops" Papalia, a notorious 73-year-old crime boss, is gunned down outside his office.

1998: Lyn Gilbank, a 52-year-old criminal lawyer and her husband are killed in their Ancaster home. Although a biker and sometime wrestler is arrested, the Crown subsequently withdraws the charges. The case remains unsolved.

Take 5 SERGEANT MARTIN SCHULENBERG'S
CRIME PREVENTION TIPS

Sergeant Martin S. Schulenberg is Crime Prevention Coordinator with Hamilton Police Service.

1. Keep your vehicles locked and consider using anti-theft locking devices. Keep all valuables out of sight.

2. Keep your doors & windows locked at your home and consider the use of security bars. Keep all entranceways clear of foliage to ensure clear visibility and eliminate hiding spots.

3. When disposing of documents, shred all personal information containing your birth date, SIN, address, phone number, credit card numbers, etc. This information can be used by perpetrators to create false accounts under your name.

4. Make sure children know their full name, address, and telephone number. Children should never let a caller at the door or on the telephone know that they are alone. They should be taught to tell a school official immediately if they see another student with a weapon.

5. Despite the advantage of having electronic pen pals, the safest advice would be not to use CHAT rooms. Always consider the risks of posting personal information and photos on web-based social and networking sites.

Take 5 HAMILTON'S TOP FIVE
CRIMES (2006)

1. **Theft under $5,000:** 8,215
2. **Assault:** 3,249
3. **Motor Vehicle Theft:** 3,133
4. **Housebreaking:** 2,269
5. **Other Break & Enter:** 1,615

Source: Hamilton Police Service.

1977: Jon Rallo, convicted of murdering his wife and two young children the previous year, is sentenced to three life terms with no parole for 25 years. Still insisting on his innocence, he is granted unescorted temporary absences by the National Parole Board in 2007.

1978: Hamilton-Wentworth Detention Centre is built to replace "The Castle," the century-old Barton Street Jail.

1980: The Discovery Train Museum, housed in 20 railway cars, is shut down after police receive a bomb threat. No bomb is found.

1980: A sniper is arrested for shooting at cars passing the Red Devils' Motorcycle Clubhouse on the Beach Strip.

Did you know...

that in 1897, a Hamilton boy named William Boylan stole a turkey from a sleigh owned by Robert Hannah, and for the crime he was sent to the Mimico Industrial School for three years?

Take 5 — FIVE FACTS ABOUT HAMILTON
CRIME STOPPERS

Since starting up in 1983 Hamilton Crime Stoppers has tracked the result of the tips received.

1. 4,306 criminal arrests have been made
2. 8,638 cases have been cleared
3. Property worth $14,718,846 has been recovered
4. Drugs valued at $62,188,999 have been seized
5. Rewards totaling $653,895 have been approved

Source: Hamilton Crime Stoppers.

1982: Elizabeth Ann Smith, wife of the chairman of the board of E.D. Smith and Co., is held hostage in her home as thieves steal more than $750,000 in jewels, furs, silver and cash. Two years later, Daniel Jurik and Norman Mark Turner are convicted and sent to jail.

1982: David Alan Burnham holds the wife and son of Ancaster bank manager John Heimbuch hostage. After injecting Janet Heimbuch with fake venom and telling her she has 35 minutes to live, Burnham calls her husband and demands $50,000 in exchange for the antidote. Burnham is sentenced to seven years in jail and ordered to make restitution.

Did you know...

that in the 1940s, prisoners from the Barton Street Jail were taken daily to work at a farm? In 1946, their crops included carrots, tomatoes, beets, parsnips, cucumbers, corn, squash and muskmelons.

Take 5 — TOP FIVE STOLEN CARS
IN 2007 (CANADA-WIDE)

1. 1999 Honda Civic SiR 2-door
2. 2000 Honda Civic SiR 2-door
3. 2004 Subaru Impreza WRX/WRX STi 4-door AWD
4. 1999 Acura Integra 2-door
5. 1994 Dodge/Plymouth Grand Caravan/Voyager

Source: Insurance Board of Canada.

1991: Nina de Villiers, a 19-year-old McMaster University student, is abducted and killed by Jonathan Yeo, a violent offender then out on bail. The following year her mother, Priscilla, establishes CAVEAT, a non-profit organization advocating "safety, peace and justice."

1992: Troy, a two-year-old German Shepherd, becomes the first Hamilton Police Canine Unit dog to die on duty. Troy distracted a gunman who was pointing a rifle at a policeman and was killed instantly.

1992: 71-year-old Holocaust survivor Morris Lax is beaten to death at his Burlington Street scrap yard. Although two suspects are arrested, charges are later withdrawn.

Did you know...

that when the need for a provincial penitentiary was first discussed in the 1830s, Hamilton was one of two locations suggested? Kingston won because of the military presence and better transportation facilities. Besides, the two commissioners making the decision were from the area.

They Said It

"Somebody's grandmother mightn't be functional, but you don't do away with her just because she isn't."

– Mayor Lloyd D. Jackson opposed suggestions to tear down the historic courthouse because it was no longer functional in the 1950s.

2001:   In the aftermath of the bombing of the World Trade Centre, a 17-year-old Sikh temple is burned to the ground. Police rule it a hate crime. The temple is subsequently rebuilt.

2005:   Art Rozendal, a 43-year-old steelworker, is beaten to death while at a restaurant with his wife and son. Two men, Cory McLeod and Kyro Sparks, are convicted and sentenced to 11 years in prison.

2007:   On February 10, fugitive Corey Rogers calls Hamilton police asking them to come and arrest him. They tell him to turn himself in at a police station. He does not. A week later, two teenagers are stabbed to death during a fight outside a bar. Rogers is arrested and charged with first-degree murder.

Did you know...

that the award-winning Hamilton Police Pipe Band is one of the oldest police bands in North America? The group was organized in 1961 for a local parade, and has been going strong ever since.

They Said It

"The scaffold at Hamilton should be demolished because it is a dangerous apparatus."

– In a fine example of gallows humor, Canadian hangman Arthur Ellis in 1938.

CRIME

Hamilton has the 7th highest crime rate of all Canadian Census Metropolitan Areas with more than 500,000 people and the 21st highest of CMAs with over 100,000. You're less likely to be murdered in Hamilton than in any other urban centre of more than half a million except Quebec City, but more likely to be robbed than in Ottawa, Quebec City or Calgary.

Source: Statistics Canada.

CRIME BY THE NUMBERS (2006)

- 21,083 criminal code incidents
- 7 homicides
- 3,249 assaults
- 676 robberies
- 3,133 motor vehicle thefts
- 1,615 break and enters
- 416 sexual offences

All violent crimes except robbery decreased between 2005 and 2006. While robbery increased by 14 percent, homicide dropped by 30 percent, attempted murder by 33 percent and assault by 21 percent.

Weblinks

Hamilton Police Services

www.hamiltonpolice.on.ca

Everything from careers and volunteering to crime files and traffic safety, find out how to get involved and stay safe.

Hamilton Crime Stoppers

www.crimestoppershamilton.com

A charitable organization run by volunteers; help them take a bite out of crime!

Hamilton police at the time, was unarmed. He saw a man on a ladder trying to get in through a second-story window and questioned him, unaware that the burglar had an accomplice. The second man shot him and Barron died of complications. The case was never solved.

Responding to a noise complaint on Sunday, September 11, 1921, Constable Reginald Pryer rode his motorcycle to the scene. When a pedestrian suddenly stepped into his path, Pryer swerved. The pedestrian was hit, although not badly injured, but the 29-year-old constable's motorcycle hit the curb, throwing Pryer headfirst into a lamppost. He succumbed to a fractured skull in hospital a few hours later.

Four years after Pryer's death, Constable Frederick Raynes, 32, was also killed in a motorcycle accident. On November 21, 1925, his sidecar collided with another vehicle, throwing Raynes into traffic where he was fatally injured.

Detective William Richard Clark and other police officers cornered an armed bank robber in a dark basement on June 27, 1929. After tear gas and other chemicals were deployed, Clark and another detective put on facemasks and entered the basement, assuming it was safe to enter the basement. The suspect killed Clark with a shotgun blast and was then shot by the second detective. Detective Clark, 36, was survived by his wife and two children.

On August 29, 1962 Constable David Richard Gregory, 26, was a beat cop who was shot and killed by a mentally unstable man who had previously killed his mother and a neighbour, then set fire to his house. The man then committed suicide.

Sergeant John Cameron McMurrich, 34, was on surveillance duty with a partner on December 22, 1968, watching gang members at a house party. Six gang members spotted them and chased them. Gunfire was exchanged, in which McMurrich and one of the gang members were killed. The other five were later arrested. McMurrich was survived by his wife and four children.

FINE, THEN

Speeding	$17.50 - $359.00
Turn Violations	$110.00
Stop Sign Violations	$110.00
Red Light Violations	$190.00
Careless Driving	$325.00
Fail To Yield Right of Way	$110.00
Following Too Closely	$110.00
Failing to Signal	$110.00
Wrong Way - One Way Street	$110.00
Disobey Road Signs	$110.00

IMPAIRED DRIVING

74,331 cases of impaired driving were reported in Canada in 2006. In 2007, Hamilton police stopped 89,536 vehicles as part of the local RIDE program. In total, there were 266 charges of impaired driving that year and 258 people charged with having a blood alcohol level of more than 0.08.

YOUTH CRIME

Approximately 74,000 youth — individuals between the ages of 12 and 17 — were charged across Canada in 2006. In every province but Quebec, the rate increased. In Hamilton, 3,077 youths were involved in crime in 2006. In 2007, the number increased by 7 percent, to 3,283.

Source: Hamilton Police Service.

CORRECTIONAL FACILITIES

The Hamilton-Wentworth Detention Centre, located on Barton Street, is a maximum security facility. The centre can accommodate up to 414 male adults and 118 young male offenders.

IN THE LINE OF DUTY

On October 27, 1903, Constable James Barron, 46, was called to the city solicitor's house to investigate a report of a prowler. Barron, like all

They Said It

"About the only good thing about Barton jail is the guards. Everything else is rotten."

– Anonymous prisoner, quoted in the *Hamilton Spectator* in the 1960s.

POLICING HAMILTON, 2007

- Number of police officers employed in Canada: 64,134
- Number of police officers employed in Hamilton: 776
- Number of citizens per officer: 669
- Number of men employed: 635
- Number of women employed: 141

In 2008, the salary for a Hamilton constable, 3rd class was $57,055. A constable 1st class earned $76,073 and a staff sergeant received $95,852.

Source: Hamilton Police Association.

STOLEN CARS

In 2006 there were 503 motor vehicles stolen for every 100,000 people in Canada. Hamilton's rate is the third lowest in Canadian CMAs with a population exceeding 500,000. You're less likely to have your car stolen in Toronto or Quebec City, but more likely to lose it in Winnipeg or Edmonton.

Did you know...

that Hamilton police responded to 85,000 calls for service in 2007 — an average of nearly ten per hour?